Never Give UP–

You're Stronger Than You Think

Books by John Mason

Be Yourself—Discover the Life You Were Meant to Live

You Can Be Your Best—Starting Today

You Can Do It—Even If Others Say You Can't

Believe You Can—The Power of a Positive Attitude

Proverbs Prayers

Never Give UP–

You're Stronger Than You Think

John Mason

Revell

a division of Baker Publishing Group
Grand Rapids, Michigan

© 2017 by John Mason

Published by Revell
a division of Baker Publishing Group
P.O. Box 6287, Grand Rapids, MI 49516-6287
www.revellbooks.com

Printed in the United States of America

Library of Congress Cataloging-in-Publication Data
Names: Mason, John, 1955– author.
Title: Never give up-you're stronger than you think / John Mason.
Description: Grand Rapids : Revell, 2017.
Identifiers: LCCN 2016051487 | ISBN 9780800727116 (pbk.)
Subjects: LCSH: Success—Religious aspects—Christianity. | Encouragement—
    Religious aspects—Christianity.
Classification: LCC BV4598.3 .M3743 2017 | DDC 158—dc23
LC record available at https://lccn.loc.gov/2016051487

In keeping with biblical principles of creation stewardship, Baker Publishing Group advocates the responsible use of our natural resources. As a member of the Green Press Initiative, our company uses recycled paper when possible. The text paper of this book is composed in part of post-consumer waste.

I am proud to dedicate this book
to my beautiful wife, Linda;
our four wonderful children,
Michelle, Greg, Mike, and Dave;
my two daughters-in-law, Brittany and Kelley;
and my three grandchildren, Emma, Olivia, and Beckett.

To Linda, for your steadfastness and love.

To Michelle, for your smarts and ability
to organize a mess like me.

To Greg, for your faith and patient perseverance.

To Mike, for your resourcefulness
and fearless approach to life.

To Dave, for that contagious smile
and how we love to watch sports together.

To Brittany and Kelley, for your love for my sons
and your love for the Lord.

To Emma, Olivia, and Beckett, for the sweetness, laughter,
and abundance of love you've brought to our family.

Your support, help, encouragement, sense of humor,
and prayers sustain and bless me every day.

Contents

PART 2: LOOKING OUTWARD 79

PART 3: LOOKING UPWARD 127

Introduction

Giving up is a region bound on the north by
compromise, on the south by indecision, on
the east by fear, and on the west by a lack of
vision.

This book is written for people who want to quit
. . . so they won't. And for people who want to go
to another level . . . so they can!

Each of us has been given a certain mixture of abilities and opportunities that make us unique. No mixture
is insignificant. Those matchless qualities that God has
placed within all of us cause us to yearn to be above
average and extraordinary.

In Genesis 3:9, God asks Adam, "Where are you?" He
is still asking that question of each of us today. Where
are we regarding God's plan for our lives? Where are we
concerning the gifts and talents He has given us?

Is God finished with you? No!

Don't leave this earth letting everyone but God use you.

It is my prayer that as you read this book, you will allow the Holy Spirit to encourage you to stay the course. Ask for God's help and never give up.

PART 1

Looking Inward

When God Sees Someone Who Doesn't Quit, He Says, "There's a Person I Can Use"

God does not quit. It's impossible for Him to do so. In Philippians 1:6 the apostle Paul wrote about "being confident of this, that he who began a good work in you will carry it on to completion until the day of Christ Jesus." There are several important points in this verse. The most crucial is the fact that God doesn't quit. Therefore, we can have great confidence that He will complete the good work He has begun in us. He will see us through every step until we reach our ultimate destination.

The majority of people quit. And that's where they stay, in the majority. The massive majority. Successful people want to be a part of the minority who would not quit.

Before any success comes, there will be opportunities to give up too soon.

Luke 18 records the story Jesus told about a persistent widow. Verse 1 says, "Jesus told his disciples [this] parable to show them that they should always pray and not give up." The psalmist David tells us, "Commit your way to the Lᴏʀᴅ, trust also in Him, and He shall bring it to pass" (Ps. 37:5 NKJV). In Galatians 6:9 we are told, "Let us not become weary in doing good, for at the proper time we will reap a harvest if we do not give up." What an incredible promise.

One of the best scriptural examples of a person who did not quit is Joseph. He had many reasons to justify giving up. When he was trapped in the pit where his jealous brothers had thrown him, I'm sure he said to himself, "This isn't the way I dreamed my life would work out!"

Later, when he was thrown into prison for a crime he didn't commit, he had an enormous opportunity to become discouraged and quit. Again he could have said to himself, "This is not right! I'm not supposed to be here." Although Joseph did not understand the steps the Lord led him through, he remained faithful to his God. Despite the trials he faced, he did not quit. Eventually, the dream that God had given him became reality. Joseph was elevated from a prisoner to a prime minister in one day!

Keep your feet on the rock when you reach the end of your rope. The only way we can lose is to quit. Quitting is a decision we make that can keep us from reaching God's goals in our lives.

It isn't always easy, but there's no greater life than that of following the Word and the will of God. Most people quit when they're on the verge of success, often when fulfillment is at their fingertips. There is only one degree of difference between hot water and steam. Don't stop one degree from your destiny. Hang on, press on, and never give up!

No Gift from God
Is Insignificant

I'd like to ask you an important question: Is God finished with you?

You may feel as if He's given up on you or that He could never use you like you once thought He could. Yet there's something deep inside of you that persistently says, "God has put me together a certain way, on purpose for a purpose, at this exact place in time." You're the most uniquely qualified and equipped person on the face of the earth to do what God has created you to do.

Don't neglect the gifts God has placed within you. It's amazing how people can devote their entire lives to fields of endeavor or to professions that have nothing to do with their inborn talents. In fact, many spend their lifetimes trying to change who God has made them. They ignore their God-given composition while constantly seeking to change their natural makeup. Instead, each of us should recognize our innate gifts, talents, and strengths and do everything in our power to build on them. You'll find that growth comes from building on talents, gifts, and strengths—not by solving problems.

One of the most important facts you can discover about God's gifts and calling in your life is that they are permanent and enduring. Romans 11:29 tells us that "the gifts and calling of God are without repentance" (KJV). The Greek word translated "repentance" in this verse literally means "irrevocable." Really grab ahold of this. Let it fully sink in. God will never recall the gifts, talents, and strengths He has given you. Even if you've never done anything with them, even if you've failed time and time again, God's gifts and calling are still resident within you. They are there this very day. Choose to do something with them, beginning right now.

God has not made us all the same. He planned you exactly how you are. His plan was for you to be different, with unique capabilities. And when it happened, it put a smile on His face! "But now God has set the members, each one of them, in the body just as He pleased" (1 Cor. 12:18 NKJV). It pleased Him to make you . . . *you.* Your individual mixture is important and valuable.

Gifts and talents are God's deposits into our personal accounts, but we determine the interest on them. The greater the amount of interest and attention we give to them, the greater their value becomes. God's gifts are not loans; they are always deposits. As such, they are never used up or depleted. In fact, the more they are used, the greater, stronger, and more valuable they become. When they are put to good use, they provide information, insight, and results that cannot be accomplished in any other way or attained from any other source. The Bible tells us this encouraging news: "God has given each of us the ability to do certain things well" (Rom. 12:6 TLB).

Each of us should make full use of all the gifts and talents that God has bestowed upon us so that we do not abound in one area while becoming bankrupt in another. There is a saying, "If the only tool you have is a hammer, you tend to treat everything like a nail." Don't make that mistake; use all of the gifts God has given you.

Never underestimate the purpose of the gifts within you. There are souls attached to your gifts. Gifts and talents are given to us not only so that we can fulfill His purpose in our own lives, but also so that we can affect people God wants to reach through us. There are people whose lives are waiting to be affected by what God has placed within you. So evaluate yourself. Define and refine your gifts, talents, and strengths. Choose today to look for opportunities to exercise your unique, God-ordained gifts and calling. Our goal at the end of our lives is to have lived so we don't have any gifts or talents remaining because we used them all.

Persistence Is a Habit—
So Is Quitting

Persistent people begin their success where most others quit. Here's a simple key to success in any area of your life: be known as a person of persistence and endurance. One person with commitment, persistence, and endurance will accomplish more than a thousand people with interest alone. "Therefore, since we are surrounded by such a great cloud of witnesses, let us throw off everything that hinders and the sin that so easily entangles. And let us run with perseverance the race marked out for us" (Heb. 12:1). The more diligently we work, the harder it is to quit.

In 1 Corinthians the apostle Paul writes, "Therefore, my beloved brethren, be steadfast, immovable, always abounding in the work of the Lord, knowing that your labor is not in vain in the Lord" (15:58 NKJV). Peter tells us, "Therefore, beloved, looking forward to these things, be diligent to be found by Him in peace, without spot and blameless" (2 Pet. 3:14 NKJV). And wise Solomon points out, "Seest thou a man diligent in his business? He shall stand before kings" (Prov. 22:29 KJV).

Many times our dreams and plans appear to be faltering. We are tempted to give up and quit trying. Instead, let's continue to water and fertilize those dreams and plans, nurturing the seeds of the vision God has placed within us. We know that if we do not quit, if we display perseverance and endurance, we will also reap a harvest (Gal. 6:9).

Far Easterners plant a tree called the Chinese bamboo. During the first four years, they water and fertilize the plant with seemingly little or no results. Then the fifth year, they again apply water and fertilizer—and in five weeks' time the tree grows ninety feet in height! This begs the question, did the Chinese bamboo tree grow ninety feet in five weeks or five years? The answer is that it grew ninety feet in five years. If at any time during those five years the people had stopped watering and fertilizing the tree, it would have died.

Charles Haddon Spurgeon said, "By perseverance the snail reached the ark." And Winston Churchill said that "the nose of a bulldog is slanted backwards so it can continue to breathe without letting go."

Never worry about how much money, ability, or equipment you start with; just begin with a million dollars' worth of determination. Remember this: it's not what you have; it's what you do with what you have that makes all the difference. Many people eagerly begin "the good fight of faith," but they forget to add patience, persistence, and endurance to their enthusiasm. Josh Billings said, "Consider the postage stamp. Its usefulness consists of the ability to stick to something until it gets there." We can learn a lot from that little ole stamp.

We Can Grow by Our Questions as Well as by Our Answers

A simple question changed the entire course of my life. Maybe the right question can change yours also.

I was a senior in high school trying to decide where I was going to go to college. Because of some successes that I had in high school, a school in the state where I lived was offering me a full scholarship just to attend their college.

There was another school that I was interested in attending that was out of state, but was offering me zero scholarships. I had attended a visitors' weekend at this university and was very impressed, and I felt that maybe there was something special there for me. But I was going to have to pay my own way, and it was also a long way from home.

The school offering the scholarship was very interested in me attending there. They called me many times asking me to commit. I was even brought there for a "recruiting" trip and was treated very well. They set it up so I could stay overnight in the dorms and experience campus life.

I'm glad that they exposed me to what it would be like to attend that college. It was probably like most other colleges, academically proud and very secular, offering most of the temptations that would get the attention of an eighteen-year-old male.

Time was of the essence, and I needed to make my decision. The college that was offering the scholarship wanted to know what I was going to do. I vividly remember walking on that campus and thinking about what I should do with my life and where I should go for college. A question came to me that was about to change my life. I remember simply asking myself, *What kind of person am I going to be four years from now if I decide on this university or the other?* After I answered that question, it became abundantly clear where I should go.

That one question and my answer changed my life. I chose the school offering no scholarship. I later received an excellent education at this university, met lifelong friends, grew spiritually, and most importantly met my wife.

I sincerely believe that God has important questions for you to ask yourself. Here are some that have helped me:

1. Am I on the path of something absolutely marvelous or something absolutely mediocre?

2. What impossible thing am I believing and planning for?

3. In what areas do I need personal development?

4. What outside influences are causing me to be better or worse?

5. Am I running *from* something or *to* something?

6. What one decision would I make if I knew it would not fail?

7. Has failure gone to my head?

8. What one thing should I eliminate from my life because it holds me back from reaching my full potential?

9. If everyone in the United States of America were on my level of spirituality, would there be a revival in the land?

10. If I'm ungrateful for what I have, how can I be happier with more?

11. Does the devil know who I am?

12. What can I do to make better use of my time?

13. Who do I need to forgive?

14. Would I recognize Jesus if I met Him on the street?

15. What good thing have I committed to do that I have quit doing?

16. Am I known for the promises I don't keep?

17. Am I becoming ordinary?

18. What is my favorite Scripture for my family, my career, and myself?

19. What is my most prevailing thought?

20. How have the people I respect earned that respect?

21. What would a genuinely creative person do in my situation?
22. How old is my attitude?
23. Does my reach exceed my grasp?
24. What gifts, talents, or strengths do I have?
25. What is one thing I can do for someone who has no opportunity to repay me?

"Give Me Six Hours to Chop Down a Tree and I Will Spend the First Four Sharpening the Axe"

All great achievers understand the value of their time. What to do and when to do it are crucial. We're all created equal in this respect: every one of us is given twenty-four hours a day. What we do with each day matters.

Make sure to take care of the two most vulnerable times in your day—the first thing in the morning and the last thing at night. It's amazing how much these two times influence the whole day. Be sure to fill them with productive words and actions. Preparation matters. Abraham Lincoln is sometimes quoted as saying, "Give me six hours to chop down a tree and I will spend the first four sharpening the axe."

I remember this story from my business school days. It demonstrates how best to use your time. We were told, "Put the big rocks in first"—plan time slots for big important tasks, otherwise urgent small demands will leave no space.

Start with a bucket, some rocks big enough to fill it, some small stones, some sand, and water.

The bucket is your available time. The rocks, stones, sand, and water are your tasks—a few big ones, some more medium-sized ones, and lots of small jobs and continuous demands and interruptions.

Put the big rocks in the bucket. Is it full?

Put the small stones in around the big rocks. Is it full?

Put the sand in and give it a shake. Is it full?

Put the water in. Now it's full.

The point is: unless you put the big rocks in first, you won't get them in at all.

In other words: plan time slots for your big issues before anything else, or the inevitable sand and water issues will fill up your days and you won't fit the big issues in.

Give your best time to your most challenging situation. It's not how much you do that matters; it's how much you finish. Here's a key: say *no*. Saying yes when you should say no is one of the biggest reasons for wasting time. One of the most valuable sayings ever coined was, "Don't spend a dollar's worth of time for ten cents' worth of results." I remember my dad telling me this many times.

I often hear people say, "I'd give anything to be able to . . ." If you have said this, you should adopt the "6 x 1 = 6" leadership principle. If you want to write a book, learn to play a musical instrument, become a better tennis player, or anything else that's important to you, then devote to it one hour a day, six days a week. Sooner than you think, your desire will become reality. You can accomplish many things in 312 hours a year! Just a commitment of one hour a day, six days a week is all it takes.

If you are saying, "I could be doing big things if I weren't so busy doing small things," then you need to take control of your time. The greater control you exercise over your time, the greater freedom you will experience. Moses prayed, "So teach us to number our days, that we may apply our hearts unto wisdom" (Ps. 90:12 KJV). The Bible teaches us that the devil comes to steal, to kill, and to destroy (John 10:10), and this verse applies to time as well as to other areas of our lives. The enemy desires to overflow us with ideas, worries, people, pleasures, and misdirections that "steal and kill and destroy" valuable time.

Don't ask time where it's gone; tell it where to go. We all have the same amount of time each day. The difference between people is determined by what they do with the amount of time at their disposal. Don't be like the airline pilot flying over the Pacific Ocean who reported to his passengers, "We're lost, but we're making great time!" Remember that the future arrives an hour at a time. Gain control of your time, and you will gain control of your life.

For Every Reason There Is to Lie, There's a Better Reason to Tell the Truth

Obey the ninth commandment. This directive is summarized in one statement: "You must not lie" (Exod. 20:16 TLB). Be a person of unquestionable integrity. Gray is never right.

It has been said that it should be easy to make an honest living because there is so little competition. Only a person with honesty and integrity can be accurately motivated or directed. Lying will always distort your ability to see God's guidance in your life. It will cause you to take steps that are not right for you. Lying will cost you more in the long term than it will save you in the short term. Bo Bennett said, "For every reason there is to lie, there's a better reason to tell the truth."

Hope built on a lie is always the beginning of loss. Never attempt to build anything on a foundation of lies and half-truths. It will not stand. Never expect God to bless a lie. In Proverbs we read, "Lying lips are an abomination to the Lord, but those who deal truthfully are His delight" (12:22 NKJV) and "A false witness will not go unpunished, and he who speaks lies shall perish" (19:9 NKJV). In Colossians the apostle Paul admonishes us: "Do not lie to one another, since you have put off the old man with his deeds, and have put on the new man who is renewed in knowledge according to the image of Him who created him" (3:9–10 NKJV).

Lying easily becomes a habit. A person who lies once will lie again with less effort. Lying is a trap. No one has a good enough memory to be a successful liar. Some good advice to remember is: "Always tell the truth, and you never have to remember what you said."

The Bible says that if you lie:

1. Your lies will come back upon you (Ps. 7:14–16).
2. You will lack understanding (Ps. 119:104).
3. You will become a fool (Prov. 10:18).
4. You will never enjoy permanent results (Prov. 12:19; 21:28).
5. You will attract liars into your life (Prov. 17:4).
6. You will be punished (Prov. 19:5).
7. You will end up in bondage (Gal. 2:4).

Little white lies grow to be big black lies. Lying is a bad seed that bears no righteous fruit. It only brings the negative in our lives.

Nugget #6

31

My wife, Linda, is the most honest person I know . . . by far. To this day, she can tell the exact moment in detail when she told her first lie (to her mother). She was four years old. She tells it like this:

> I was bored and wanted a friend to play with. A friend lived next door. My mother was in our backyard, hanging laundry on the clothesline to dry in the sun.
>
> I looked up at her and said, "Jimmy invited me over to play."
>
> She looked down at me over her left shoulder and said something like, "No, he didn't, did he?"
>
> I looked sheepish. I got sent inside the house. I didn't get to play with my friend or even play outside in the sunshine.
>
> I never lied to her again.

It was so out of character for her; it must have shown all over her face, because her mother responded to her immediately. She's so committed to the truth that even today that story makes her uncomfortable and embarrassed.

Determine to be free from the bondage of breaking the ninth commandment; determine to always tell the truth.

Honestly, is there any other way to live?

Be Decisive, Even If It Means You'll Sometimes Be Wrong

Indecision is deadly. Some of the most miserable people are those who can never make a decision. When the mind is in doubt, it is easily swayed by slight impulses, opening the door to many wrong decisions. Many times indecision causes things to go from bad to worse. The middle of the road is a dangerous place to be.

It's better to be decisive and miss every once in a while than to be so indecisive that when you're finally right, the opportunity is long gone.

Our challenge? To be decisive dreamers. Harry Truman is quoted as saying, "Some questions cannot be answered, but they can be decided." Even when we do not have all the facts available, we usually have all the facts needed to make a decision. The Bible says to let the peace of God rule in our hearts (Col. 3:15). The Amplified Version tells us to let the peace that comes from Christ "act as [an] umpire" in our hearts. God's peace can say "safe" to an idea or say "out" to a relationship.

If you are neutral on spiritual matters, eventually you'll find yourself operating against heaven. Thank God we serve a decisive Lord. He has given us His peace and His Word so that we can make wise decisions. We should not be the kind of people who claim that God has told us one thing this week and the very opposite next week. God does not change in such quick degrees, nor does He ever direct anyone to act contrary to the good sense and sound judgment shown in His Word.

God wants us to be decisive. As His children, we should be like our heavenly Father, with whom there is "no variableness, neither shadow of turning" (James 1:17 KJV). We should be people of deep conviction. If the devil controls our will, he controls our destiny. But if God controls our will, then He controls our destiny.

Stop the negative by being decisive.

Lawyers should never ask a grandma a question if they aren't prepared for the answer. In a trial in Mississippi, a Southern small-town prosecuting attorney called his first witness to the stand—a grandmotherly, elderly woman. He approached her and asked, "Mrs. Jones, do you know me?"

She responded, "Why, yes, I do know you, Mr. Williams. I've known you since you were a boy, and frankly you've been a big disappointment to me. You lie, you cheat on your wife, and you manipulate people and talk about them behind their backs. You think you're a big shot, when you haven't got the brains to realize you'll never amount to anything more than a two-bit paper pusher. Yes, I know you."

The lawyer was stunned. Not knowing what else to do, he pointed across the room and asked, "Mrs. Jones, do you know the defense attorney?"

She again replied, "Why, yes, I do. I've known Mr. Bradley since he was a youngster too. He's lazy and bigoted, and he has a drinking problem. He can't build a healthy relationship with anyone, and his law practice is one of the worst in the entire state . . . not to mention, he cheated on his wife with three different women. One of them was your wife. Yes, I know him."

The defense attorney nearly died on the spot.

The judge asked both counselors to approach the bench and, in a very quiet voice, said, "If either of you idiots ask her if she knows me, I'll send you both to the electric chair."

Better to be decisive than to suffer the consequences of indecision.

Be the most decisive person you know. Leaders should have wills, not wishes. The Bible says, "A double-minded man is unstable in all his ways" (James 1:8 KJV). An indecisive person allows instability to creep into every area of life. If we don't decide what is important to us, we will do only what is important to others. A greater degree of wishful thinking leads to a greater degree of mediocrity. Being decisive, being focused, and committing ourselves to the fulfillment of a dream significantly increases our probability of success while closing the door to wrong options.

A person with one watch knows what time it is; a person with two watches is never quite sure. The choice is ours. Let's be decisive. Don't be a person who says, "My decision is maybe, and that's final."

Focus on What to Do Next Instead of Thinking about What Went Wrong

Get rid of any "loser's limp" you're still walking around with! God's amazing grace and power can break the power of the past to dominate our present and influence our future. Don't consume your tomorrows by feeding on your yesterdays. Realize you're living in the "good old days" now. Say good-bye to your past. There is not one single thing you can do about it. It is gone.

No one wakes up in the morning and proclaims, "Today I'm going to gain weight." You know the reality; the extra pounds gradually add up over time. Then, while trying on a pair of pants you haven't worn for a year, you notice they are much tighter than you remember. The same is true about accumulating the "weight" of the past. You never got over the job you thought you deserved. Your spouse hurt you. A business associate took advantage of you.

No one can carry the weight of the past. It slows you down, makes you want to quit, and tires you out. You need to let go of the past so it doesn't:

1. Get you off course. Thoughts of revenge or what might have been are some of the most unproductive thoughts you can have. While you're thinking this way, you're not planning or dreaming about your future.

2. Typecast you. You see yourself as a person who failed, made the critical mistake, or went the wrong direction. No wonder you begin to believe you're a loser. And note that you're mostly attracting other "losers."

3. Sour your outlook. The future looks bad no matter how good things really are. Every part of your life picks up the stick of your rotten attitude.

4. Wipe you out. It takes a lot of effort to carry the past, pay for today, and provide for the future. God never set us up to do this. Clinging to your past makes it very hard to step into your future. You're tired, and it feels like you don't have the energy to do what it takes to move forward. So, you stay where you are: sad, fatigued, and discouraged.

Jesus said, "No one, having put his hand to the plow, and looking back, is fit for the kingdom of God" (Luke 9:62 NKJV). If we are not careful, we will allow the past to hold us. The more we look backward, the less we are able to see forward. The past does not determine what God can do for us today or tomorrow.

That is the beauty of the Christian life. Even when we fail, we can ask for forgiveness and be totally cleansed of and released from our past actions. Whatever the past holds against you can be broken. It is never God who holds us back. We hold ourselves back by allowing the past to keep us from living to the fullest in the present and future. Failure is waiting around the corner for those who live off of yesterday's successes and failures. Choose to be forward-focused, not past-possessed. Learn to profit from the past while investing in the future.

The apostle Paul wrote:

> Brethren, I count not myself to have apprehended: but this one thing I do, forgetting those things which are behind, and reaching forth unto those things which are before, I press toward the mark for the prize of the high calling of God in Christ Jesus. (Phil. 3:13–14 KJV)

I've found four keys to letting go of the past. First, stop feeling sorry for yourself. You probably played a part in your disappointments. And life's not fair anyway. Also, don't forget the times you got a break you didn't deserve. They will probably outnumber the negative breaks.

Second, decide to stop investing your time in past thinking. It's an investment that pays no return.

Third, focus on today. The only thing you really control is what you do every day. This moment counts. Thinking about today will take you out of your past.

Finally, forgive. Forgive yourself. Forgive those who, by their actions, keep you living in the past. This is the ultimate power of the past . . . forgiveness. Let go and go on.

The key is "forgetting those things which are behind" in order to reach for "the high calling of God in Christ Jesus." To fulfill your calling in Christ, you must first forget past failures and mistakes. Today is the day to shake off the shackles of the past and to move forward.

The past is past.

Some People Wait Their Entire Lives for Their Ship to Come In, Not Realizing They Are Standing in an Airport

Procrastination is a killer.

When you kill time, you begin to kill the ideas and directions God placed within you. *The Living Bible*'s paraphrase of Ecclesiastes 11:4 says, "If you wait for perfect conditions, you will never get anything done." The best time of day is now.

Let's be like the apostles. Even today, they are not known for their policies, procedures, theories, or excuses, but for their *acts*. Many people say they are waiting for God, but in most cases God is waiting for them. The cost of growth is always less than the cost of stagnation. As

Edmund Burke said, "The only thing necessary for the triumph of evil is for good men to do nothing."

Occasionally you may notice someone who doesn't do anything yet seems to have some success in life. Don't be deceived; things are never as they appear. Remember the old saying, "Even a broken clock is right twice a day." As Christians, we are called to make progress—not excuses.

The first step to overcoming procrastination is to eliminate all excuses for not taking immediate action.

The second step is to be less busy. Everyone is always on the move. People are moving forward, backward, and sometimes nowhere at all as though they are on a treadmill. The mistake most people make is thinking that the main goal of life is to stay busy. Such thinking is a trap. What is important is not whether you are busy but whether you are progressing. The question is one of activity versus accomplishment.

A gentleman named Jean-Henri Fabre conducted an experiment with processionary caterpillars, so named for their habit of blindly following each other. In his experiment, Fabre placed these tiny creatures in a circle. For twenty-four hours the caterpillars dutifully followed one another around and around and around. Then Fabre placed the caterpillars around a saucer full of pine needles (their favorite food). For six days, the mindless creatures moved around and around the saucer, finally dying from starvation and exhaustion even though an abundance of choice food was located less than two inches away. For all their activity, the caterpillars accomplished nothing.

Be a person who accomplishes great things for God—not talks about it. Procrastinators are good at talking, not doing. Mark Twain said, "Noise produces nothing. Often a hen who has merely laid an egg cackles as though she has laid an asteroid."

Procrastination is a tool of the devil to hold us back and to make us miss God's timing in our lives. "The desire of the lazy man kills him, for his hands refuse to labor" (Prov. 21:25 NKJV). The longer we take to act on God's direction, the more unclear it becomes. So take action—now.

Fear Isn't Reality

Fear is a poor chisel for carving out tomorrow. If you're worried about tomorrow, I have good news for you: Worry isn't reality! Worry is really the triumph of fear over faith.

An old Swedish proverb says, "Worry gives a small thing a big shadow." Worry is simply the misuse of the creative imagination God has placed within us. The word *worry* is derived from an Anglo-Saxon term meaning "to strangle" or "to choke off." There is no question that worry and fear choke off the positive creativity God gives us.

There is a story about a woman who cried profusely while standing on a street corner. A man came up to her and asked why she was weeping. The woman shook her head and replied, "I was just thinking that maybe someday I would get married. We would later have a beautiful baby girl. Then one day this child and I would go for a walk along this street, and my darling daughter would run into the street, get hit by a car, and die."

It sounds like a pretty ridiculous situation—weeping because of something that will probably never happen. Yet we act this way when we worry. We blow a situation out of proportion that might never come to pass.

A taxi passenger tapped the driver on the shoulder to ask him a question. The driver screamed, lost control of the car, nearly hit a bus, went up on the sidewalk, and stopped inches from the front window of a store.

For a second, everything went quiet in the cab. Then the driver said, "Look, buster, don't ever do that again. You scared the living daylights out of me!"

The passenger apologized and said, "I didn't realize that a little tap would scare you so much."

The driver replied, "Sorry, it's not really your fault. Today is my first day as a cabdriver. I've been driving a funeral van for the last twenty-five years."

Fear and worry are like interest paid in advance on something you may never own. Would you pay interest in advance on a house you know you'd never move into? Would you pay interest in advance on a car you know you'd never drive? Of course not! But isn't that the way fear and worry try to steal from our lives?

Things are seldom as they seem. "Skim milk masquerades as cream," said W. S. Gilbert. As we dwell on matters beyond our control, an adverse effect sets in. Too much analysis always leads to paralysis.

When fear rises in our minds, we should *expect the opposite* in our lives. We should expect faith to rise in our hearts to shield us against worrisome thoughts. Faith is the opposite of fear. Yet they are both a lot alike. They both believe that what you cannot see will come to pass. Trust faith. Put your faith in God, not in fear.

The Bible says, "Cast your burden on the Lord, and He shall sustain you; He shall never permit the righteous to be moved" (Ps. 55:22 NKJV). Never respond out of fear, and never fear to respond. Action attacks fear; inaction reinforces it.

Don't worry and don't fear. Instead, take your fear and worry to the Lord, "casting all your care upon Him, for He cares for you" (1 Pet. 5:7 NKJV). Picture your fears, like a fishing line, being cast a long way away from you into God's hands. Leave your worries there. He loves and cares for you.

Worry is a route that leads from somewhere to nowhere. Never let it direct your life.

Our Words Create Our Worlds

Recently I saw a sign under a mounted large-mouth bass. It read: "If I had kept my mouth shut, I wouldn't be here." How true! Don't jump into trouble mouth first. What we say is important. The book of Job reminds us, "How forcible are right words" (6:25 KJV).

We Christians should be known as those who speak positively, speak the Word of God into situations, and speak forth words of life.

What we say is important. The Bible says that "out of the abundance of the heart the mouth speaks" (Matt. 12:34 NKJV). We need to change our vocabulary; we need to speak words of life and light. Our talk should always line up with the Word of God.

We shouldn't be like the man who joined a monastery where the monks were allowed to speak only two words every seven years. After the first seven years had passed, the man met with the abbot, who asked him, "Well, what are your two words?"

"Food's bad," replied the man.

Seven years later the clergyman asked, "What are your two words now?"

"Bed's hard," the man responded.

Seven years later—twenty-one years after he entered the monastery—the man met with the abbot for the third and final time. "And what are your two words this time?" the abbot asked.

"I quit."

"Well, I'm not surprised," the cleric answered disgustedly. "All you've done since you got here is complain!"

Don't be like that man; don't be known as a person whose only words are negative. The most influential person you will talk to all day is you. So, you should be very careful what you say to you.

What you're claiming has a way of reaching back and claiming you. Proverbs 18:21 is true: "Death and life are in the power of the tongue" (KJV).

If you are a member of the "murmuring grapevine," you need to resign. Our Lord instructed His disciples, "Do not murmur among yourselves" (John 6:43 NKJV). The apostle Paul exhorted the believers of his day:

> Do all things without complaining and disputing, that you may become blameless and harmless, children of God without fault in the midst of a crooked and perverse generation, among whom you shine as lights in the world. (Phil. 2:14–15 NKJV)

Our words are seeds planted into other people's lives. Contrary to what you may have heard, talk is not cheap. Talk is expensive! What we say affects what we get from others and what others get from us. When we speak wrongly, we diminish our ability to see and hear the will of God. But when we speak positive, God-filled words, they bring life to all.

Let me pose this question for you: Starting Monday, what would happen if you changed what you said about your biggest problem, your biggest opportunity? Our words create our worlds. Your words have the power to start fires or quench passion.

Choices Bring Increase or Decrease

We make choices every day. We are given options. What we choose can bring increase or decrease. What will you decide?

- Overcoming evil versus tolerating evil
- Saying "how I can" versus "if I can"
- Growing better versus bitter
- Saying "get up" versus "give up"
- Decisiveness versus indifference
- Enthusiasm versus lukewarmness
- God-led risk versus man-made security
- Choice versus chance
- Peace versus strife
- Standing out versus blending in

- How much I get done versus how much I attempt to do
- Development versus stagnation
- Obtaining versus complaining
- Determination versus discouragement
- Priorities versus aimlessness
- Growth versus death
- Demanding more of yourself versus excusing yourself
- Doing for others versus doing for ourselves
- Being selected to be in a who's who versus asking, "Why me?"
- Opposing darkness versus coexisting with darkness
- Progressing versus drifting
- Solutions versus problems
- Action versus activity
- Committing versus trying
- Accountability versus irresponsibility
- More of God versus more of everything else

Never Start Your Day in Neutral

*E*xciting, innovative, transforming, productive—words that will never be associated with neutrality. Lukewarmness, indifference, apathy, defensiveness, coldness, a lack of interest—attitudes no one wants to be around.

Never let your quest for "balance" in life become an excuse for refusing the unique, productive, invading move God directs you to take. Many times the attempt to maintain balance is really just an excuse for remaining lukewarm. Three times the Lord said to Joshua, "Be strong and courageous" (Josh. 1:6, 7, 9). I believe He is saying that to each one of us today.

Here's a great opportunity. Choose to be a person who is on the offensive, not the defensive. Never try to defend your present position and situation. People who live defensively never rise above average. Decide to be on the offensive, to take the initiative. Lukewarm, uninvolved people are never secure regardless of their wealth, education, or position.

Thinking on the offensive and taking the initiative are the master keys that open doors of opportunity in your life. Create a habit of taking the initiative and *never start your day in neutral.* Every morning when your feet hit the floor, think on the offensive, move forward, and take control of your day and your life.

When you choose to live on the offensive, the atmosphere of your life will begin to change. If you don't like the tone of your life, decide to take the offensive position and watch what happens. "Taking the offensive" starts by making an inward decision that inspires an outward action.

When you choose to act on the offensive, keep all your conflicts impersonal. Fight the issue, not the person. Speak about what God within you can do, not about what others are incapable of doing. You will find that when all of your reasons are defensive, your cause will almost never succeed. A basketball team that never takes a shot never wins a game.

Pulling back and thinking defensively usually enhances a problem. Intimidation always precedes defeat. If you aren't sure which way to go, pray and move toward the situation in faith.

Be like the two fishermen trapped in a storm in the middle of a lake. One turned to the other and asked, "Should we pray or should we row?"

His wise companion responded, "Let's do both!"

That's taking the offensive!

A Goal Changes Everything

Give a man a basketball and tell him to shoot, and his response will be, "At what?" When there is no goal, there is no purpose for shooting. He could shoot the ball anywhere, and wherever it landed would be the result. Not much to it.

On the other hand, if you give the man a hoop and challenge him to throw the ball in the hoop, everything changes. You have now given him something to aim at, something to test his skills against, something to measure his progress with, and something that gives all of his effort *purpose*. All by adding in a simple goal.

That's what a goal does to a person's life—it changes everything.

In Habakkuk the Lord tells the prophet, "Write the vision and make it plain on tablets, that he may run who reads it" (2:2 NKJV). This Scripture reveals the key to successful goal setting.

Your vision must be written. When you keep a vision in your mind, it isn't really a goal; it is nothing more than a dream. There is power in putting that dream on paper. When you commit something to writing, commitment to achievement naturally follows.

God wrote His vision for us in the form of the Bible. He doesn't rely only on the Holy Spirit to guide us; He put His directions in writing. When the vision is written down clearly, "He may run who reads it."

The key word is *run*. God desires that we run with the vision for our lives. As long as we're running with the vision, we won't turn around. When we walk with a vision, it's easy to change directions and go the wrong way. We can't stroll to a goal.

In Proverbs 24 we read, "Any enterprise is built by wise planning, becomes strong through common sense, and profits wonderfully by keeping abreast of the facts" (vv. 3–4 TLB). Simply stated, effective goal setting provides an opportunity to bring the future to the present. That way you can run with it today. You will find that achievement is easy when your outer goals become inner commitments.

Even though we have the Holy Spirit, we still need to prepare; He just makes us better equipped to do so. God doesn't desire for us to be disorderly or to waste funds. That's why proper planning is so important. Plan for potential. Believe for God's biggest dream. When you plan, look to the future, not to the past. You can't effectively drive forward when you're looking out the rear window.

We all have an opportunity for success. Having a bad life requires as much energy (maybe more) as having a good life, yet most people live aimless lives because they never decide to write down their vision and then follow through. If you cannot see the mark, you cannot press toward it.

Always involve yourself with something bigger than you are because that's where God is. At its beginning, every great success seemed impossible.

"Ponder the path of your feet, and let all your ways be established" (Prov. 4:26 NKJV). You will find that what you learn on the path to your goals is actually more valuable than achieving the goal itself. Columbus discovered America while searching for a route to India. Be on the lookout for the "Americas" in your path. Put God's vision for your life on paper, and begin to run with His plan.

Bark Less, Wag More

Smile—it adds to your face value!

Christians should be the happiest, most enthusiastic people on earth. In fact, the word *enthusiasm* comes from the Greek word *entheous*, which means "God within" or "full of God."

The bigger the challenge you're facing, the more enthusiasm you need. Philippians 2:5 says, "Have the same mindset as Christ Jesus." I believe that Jesus was a man who had a smile on His face and a spring in His step.

Smiling—proof that you are happy and enthusiastic—is always a choice, not a result. It is a decision you must consciously make. Enthusiasm and joy and happiness will improve your personality and people's opinion of you. It will help you keep a proper perspective on life. Helen Keller said, "Keep your face to the sunshine, and you cannot see the shadow."

Our attitude always tells others what we expect in return.

I am so thankful I have a wonderful marriage. My wife, Linda, and I are exact opposites, but we have found a way to laugh almost every day since we were married in 1977. Through fun days and not-so-fun days, laughter has kept us close. It's helped us look past our differences to the good (and funny) in nearly every situation. It's true that if you can laugh at it, you can live with it. If you can laugh together, you can stay together.

A smile is a powerful weapon. It can break the ice in tough situations. You will find that being enthusiastic is like having a cold; both are very contagious. A laugh a day will keep negative people away. As enthusiasm increases, stress and fear decrease. The Bible says that the joy of the Lord is our strength (Neh. 8:10).

Many people say, "Well, no wonder those people are happy, confident, and positive; if I had their job and assets, I would be happy too!" Such thinking falsely assumes that successful people are positive because they have a good income and lots of possessions. But the reverse is true. Such people probably have a good income and lots of possessions as a result of being positive, confident, and happy.

Enthusiasm always inspires action. No significant accomplishment has ever been made without enthusiasm. In John 15:10–11 we have a promise from the Lord that says, "If you keep my commands, you will remain in my love, just as I have kept my Father's commands and remain in his love. I have told you this so that my joy may be in you and that your joy may be complete."

Add a smile to everything you wear today!

Alibis Are Lies Gift Wrapped in Explanations

Excuses are for people who don't want it bad enough. Stop saying, *I'll try, maybe later, I can't, I won't, I don't have the time,* or *I might.* Instead, start saying, *I can, I will,* and *I won't give up.* Eat your excuses for breakfast, and go forward.

Quitting, giving up, failing, and even judging—all of these begin with an excuse. Never allow an obstacle in your life to become an alibi. "You, therefore, have no excuse, you who pass judgment on someone else, for at whatever point you judge another, you are condemning yourself, because you who pass judgment do the same things" (Rom. 2:1). Be a person who makes progress, not excuses.

There have always been individuals who have made up excuses to the Lord. Some knew their alibis weren't true, while others actually believed their own excuses. Never let your excuses be greater than your dreams.

Jesus told a parable of the great end times banquet and the men who were invited to the Lord's Table:

> But they all alike began to make excuses. The first said, "I have just bought a field, and I must go and see it. Please excuse me."
>
> Another said, "I have just bought five yoke of oxen, and I'm on my way to try them out. Please excuse me."
>
> Still another said, "I just got married, so I can't come." (Luke 14:18–20)

These men made excuses and missed out on salvation. All of them made the mistake of believing their alibis rather than God.

Moses and Gideon made excuses to the Lord, yet they recognized that their excuses were not the truth. When the Lord sent Moses to Pharaoh, Moses said:

> "Pardon your servant, Lord. I have never been eloquent, neither in the past nor since you have spoken to your servant. I am slow of speech and tongue."
>
> The LORD said to him, "Who gave human beings their mouths? Who makes them deaf or mute? Who gives them sight or makes them blind? Is it not I, the LORD? Now go; I will help you speak and will teach you what to say." (Exod. 4:10–12)

When the Lord asked Gideon to save Israel from their invaders, Gideon argued:

> "But how can I save Israel? My clan is the weakest in Manasseh, and I am the least in my family." The LORD

answered, "I will be with you, and you will strike down all the Midianites, leaving none alive." (Judg. 6:15–16)

Do not hide behind an excuse. Jesus said, "If I had not come and spoken to them, they would not be guilty of sin; but now they have no excuse for their sin" (John 15:22). An alibi will always keep you from completing the assignment God has for you.

Nobody cares about your excuses. No one pities you and your alibis. No one is going to pamper you in your hazy halfheartedness. Say good-bye to that alibi.

Quit making excuses, putting it off, complaining about it, dreaming about it, whining about it, crying about it, believing you can't, worrying if you can, waiting until you're older, skinnier, richer, braver, or all-around better. Suck it up, hold on tight, say a prayer, make a plan, and just do it.

Don't Quit after a Victory

The two most likely times for people to quit something is after a defeat *and* after a victory. Recognize this fact, and you will quit less and continue further.

I experienced this truth firsthand. No one was more surprised than me about the success of my first book, *An Enemy Called Average*. I definitely experienced a victory after that self-published book sold more than one hundred thousand copies the first year. Seeing and hearing the changes the book brought into so many lives inspired me to keep writing. Writing that first book was very hard for me—in fact, it took me nearly two and a half years. But rather than quit after this victory, all I wanted to do was more.

I knew that the work was going to be hard for me and that it was going to take many evenings and many weekends to write the second book. In spite of all that, there was no way I was going to quit after the victory of my first book. I was determined to write a better book in a shorter period of time, a book that would reach as many or more people as the first one. In less than a year, my second book, *You're Born an Original—Don't Die a Copy*, was released. Now nineteen books later, with nearly two million copies sold, I'm so glad I didn't quit after that victory.

One of the great prizes of victory is the opportunity to do more. The trouble is that small doses of success have often inoculated us from catching the big victory.

I'm a big sports fan. I've always observed that a team that's overjoyed to make it to the semifinals rarely wins the championship. The championship team appreciates a victory but isn't satisfied. Its only goal is to win it all; that's why they nearly always prevail.

Robert Schuller said, "Don't cash in; cast into deeper water." Do not stop after a success; keep the forward momentum. Don't stop after a failure; dust yourself off, learn the lesson, and start up again.

The Bible offers us God's kind of momentum and growth. Here are His ways to keep going:

- Be generous (2 Cor. 9:9).
- Speak the truth (Eph. 4:15).
- Be spiritually mature (Heb. 6:1).
- Crave the Word of God (1 Pet. 2:2).
- Grow in the grace and knowledge of Jesus (2 Pet. 3:18).

God's definition of spiritual momentum is found in this passage:

For this very reason, make every effort to add to your faith goodness; and to goodness, knowledge; and to knowledge, self-control; and to self-control, perseverance; and to perseverance, godliness; and to godliness, mutual affection; and to mutual affection, love. For if you possess these qualities in increasing measure, they will keep you from being ineffective and unproductive in your knowledge of our Lord Jesus Christ. (2 Pet. 1:5–8)

Picture a large boulder at the top of a hill. This boulder represents our lives. If we rock the boulder back and forth and get it moving, its momentum will make it almost unstoppable. The same is true for us.

Here's a clear way to remember this truth: let go of whatever makes you stop in a victory or a defeat.

The Price of Greatness Is Responsibility

One of the biggest lies we believe is that we are not responsible for our own actions. We blame our mothers, our employers, our neighbors, the government, or society. But the Bible clearly indicates who is responsible and accountable for our deeds: "So then every one of us shall give account of himself to God" (Rom. 14:12 KJV).

We may attempt to shift the blame to others, but there is no escaping the truth: every time we point a finger at someone else, three fingers point back at us. Don't blame anyone or anything for the circumstances you find yourself in. If you do that, you are saying you are powerless over your own life. Winston Churchill said, "The price of greatness is responsibility."

Accept responsibility for your actions. Be accountable for your results. Take ownership of your mistakes. "The moment you take responsibility for everything in your life is the moment you can change anything in your life" (Hal Elrod).

I believe that God wants us to learn most things for ourselves because what we learn for ourselves stays with us deeper and longer than anything we learn from others. Mark Twain wrote, "A man who carries a cat by the tail learns something he can learn no other way."

Throughout my early career as a consultant, I met many businesspeople who were looking for answers. I was amazed to see how many were anxiously searching for help from other people when they had everything they needed to succeed. They were willing to give up control of their vision to others in exchange for money, or simply because they didn't want to be alone. It isn't always easy for leaders to be by themselves. Their mistake was in looking to others instead of looking to God. The false sense of security they found in others led them to unbalanced relationships; relationships that eventually resulted in the destruction of their dreams.

God sends people across our paths to bless and help us, but we should be directed by God and very cautious when entering into any partnership. We must be sure that the reason for the relationship is right and sure that we aren't merely looking for a shortcut.

For every successful partnership, there are hundreds of disasters. Exercise great caution when you affiliate with someone else. In Exodus, God gave Moses some good advice that is applicable to Christians today. He said, "Be careful not to make a treaty with those who live in the land where you are going, or they will be a snare among you" (Exod. 34:12).

Nugget #18

Faith is like a toothbrush: everyone should have it and use it every day, but we shouldn't use someone else's. Decide for yourself. Learn for yourself. Answer for yourself.

Accept responsibility for your life. "Take responsibility and initiative for yourself. Stop blaming your circumstances on what you are able to change" (Sonya Teclai). Know that it is you who will get you where you want to go, no one else. The best helping hand you will find is at the end of your own arm.

A Mistake Is Temporary—
Quitting Is Forever

We all experience failure and make mistakes. In fact, successful people always have more failure in their lives than average people do. Great people throughout history have all failed at some point in their lives.

It is always better to fail in doing something than to excel at doing nothing. A flawed diamond is more valuable than a perfect brick. People who have no failures also have few victories.

I am somewhat of an expert at making mistakes. I remember one doozy of a mistake that caused me to forever change how I prepare for my trips.

I had waited until the last minute to get ready for a trip to speak at a church halfway across the country. I was up late at night preparing and packing for an early morning flight. Candidly, it was a mad scramble.

The early morning alarm rang and I got up to put some last-minute items into my luggage, then off I hustled to the airport. I was scheduled to speak twice at a church I had never been to before, for a pastor I had never met.

The flight was uneventful until about thirty minutes before I was scheduled to land. I began to have an uneasy feeling. You know the kind of feeling, like you left the door unlocked, or the iron plugged in, or perhaps as a guest speaker you forgot your Bible.

Yes, I had forgotten my Bible. A not-so-mild panic began to run through me. Here I was flying in to speak for this pastor and his congregation. At a church I'd never been to, for a pastor I'd never met. I sure didn't want to come up to him the first time, introduce myself, and say, "Nice to meet you, Pastor. My name is John Mason. May I borrow your Bible?"

I thought this pastor would look at me and think, *Who is this person I've entrusted to speak at my church? He doesn't even have a Bible!*

So, I decided I'd quickly look for a Bible in the airport before I met the pastor in the baggage claim area. I was desperate. I thought, *Maybe there's a Bible here at the airport, although I've never seen one in any of the airport bookstores before.* I hurriedly went from one end of the terminal to the other searching for a Bible.

As fortune would have it, the last place I looked, I asked the clerk, "Do you stock Bibles?"

"Yes," she said, "we have a Bible." She went over to the shelf in the remotest corner of the store and pulled out a white "wedding/baptismal gift" Bible.

Now I was thinking, *I didn't bring white shoes, white pants, and a white tie. I can't preach from this white Bible.* But I was desperate, so I went ahead and bought it.

By now, I was late to meet with the pastor in baggage claim. It was pretty clear to me who the pastor was, because he was searching all over a rather empty claim area for someone. So, I went up to him and said, "Hello, Pastor. I'm John Mason."

We got my luggage and put it in his car. We began to travel to what I thought would be my hotel. But after a moment or two in the car, the pastor turned to me and said, "John, would you like to go over to the church first? I'd like to show you around."

I thought for a second, *Yes! I'd love to go to the church . . . Churches have Bibles!* So I told him right away, "I'd love to go to your church."

We arrived at a beautiful church building. We began to walk into the front foyer on our way to the sanctuary. He was walking two or three steps ahead of me. Right before we entered the sanctuary, there was a large box off to my right with a sign above it that said Lost and Found. I got excited. I looked inside that box, and wouldn't you know it, inside that box was a beautiful Bible. So, I "found" that Bible. Picked it up and took it with me.

That whole weekend I preached from that beautiful found Bible. But in the back of my mind I kept thinking, *Somebody's looking at me out in the congregation thinking,* That guy's got my Bible!

See, I told you I know about mistakes.

How do you respond to failure and mistakes? Failure doesn't mean nothing has been accomplished; there is always the opportunity to learn something. Always remember that God isn't surprised by your stumbles. His love, grace, mercy, and forgiveness are bigger than any mess you make.

Those who don't expect anything are the ones who are never disappointed. Those who never try never fail. Anyone who is currently achieving anything in life is simultaneously risking failure. If you're not prepared to be wrong, you'll never accomplish anything great.

You will get knocked down; it is how fast you get up that makes all the difference. There is a positive correlation between spiritual maturity and how quickly a person responds to failures and mistakes. Individuals who are spiritually mature have a greater ability to get up and go on than people who are spiritually immature. The less mature the person, the longer they hold on to past failures.

Here is the key to getting free from the stranglehold of past failures and mistakes: Learn the lesson and forget the details. Gain from the experience, but do not roll the minute details of it over and over in your mind. Build on the experience, and move forward in your life.

God never sees any of us as failures; He only sees us as learners. We fail only when we don't learn from each experience. The decision is up to us—we can choose to turn a failure into a hitching post or a guidepost in our lives. When you get knocked down, get back up.

Remember that the call is higher than the fall.

Take a Chance—
It Might Give You
a Brand-New Life

Some of the best things that have ever happened to you in life happened because you said yes to something daring at the time. Instead of staying where you were, you chose to go somewhere else.

Learn to stretch and reach out to where God is. Aim high and take risks. The world's approach is to look to next year based on last year. We Christians need to reach for the potential, not base our success on the past. Those who make great strides are those who take chances and plan toward the challenges of life.

Don't become so caught up in the small matters that you cannot take advantage of significant opportunities. Most people spend their entire lives letting down buckets into empty wells and then waste their days trying to pull them up again and again.

People whose faith runs ahead of their minds make all the great discoveries. Significant achievements have been obtained by taking large risks on important issues and not minimal risks on minor issues. The fact that you are reading this (my nineteenth) book is a direct result of me doing something I *never* thought possible.

Back in the late 1980s, I began to have a very unexpected enormous thought. That thought was, *I should write a book*. Before that, I had never considered doing writing of any kind. In fact, if you would've interviewed me when I was in college and asked me to list fifty things I might do with my life, standing and speaking in front of people would be on that list but writing a book would not be found anywhere. Yet I had this persistent idea, or you might say, direction, to write a book.

So, I did what any reasonable person would do. I went out and bought a book on how to write a book. In fact, it was the most famous book on writing at that time, *The Elements of Style*. After I read that book, I became even more convinced that I absolutely could not write a book. But this idea would not go away.

Then something interesting happened. God sent some people across my path. When God gets ready to bless your life, He sends people into your life. A couple who I respected met with me. I told them, "I had a crazy idea that I was supposed to write a book, but now I'm convinced I really can't do it."

Immediately, they looked at me and said, "John, you should do it, but you need to be yourself. You like to tell stories, share short expressions, and add humor to almost everything you do. You should write a book like that." Suddenly, I had hope. I believed.

I immediately thought, *Yes, I can do that kind of book*; so I began my impossible idea. It took me nearly two and a half years to complete my first book. I vividly remember typing the last words into my Apple IIc computer at 4:30 in the morning, sobbing, falling into bed. My first book, *An Enemy Called Average*, was finished.

I had written the book that was on my heart. A book that was truly me. My faith was running way ahead of my mind. I knew that nearly three hundred thousand books are published every year and that 70 percent of all books purchased are never read. But I was hopeful and full of faith that maybe this book would be different.

The publisher that I worked for at the time was very clear with me that they would never promote my book in any way and had no interest in publishing my book, only distributing it. They would graciously list it on an order form along with over seven hundred other titles. I was happy. I had no idea what God was about to do.

With zero promotion and only a title line listed on an eight-page order form, the book began to sell like crazy by word of mouth. It sold so many copies that within three months the publisher came to me and wanted to publish it; they were excited.

I told them no. I had taken all the risk and wanted to go forward on my own. It later sold over one hundred thousand copies that first year and at the time of this writing has sold over six hundred thousand copies and been translated into more than thirty languages. My nineteen books in total have sold nearly two million copies. That's one book for every mile around the equator eighty times! No one is more surprised than me.

Nugget #20

I took a chance on an impossible idea from God, and it changed my life. You can too.

Choose to dream big, to strive to reach the full potential of your calling. Choose to major on the important issues of life, not on the unimportant. H. Stern said, "If you're hunting rabbits in tiger country, you must keep your eye peeled for tigers, but when you are hunting tigers, you can ignore the rabbits." There are plenty of tigers to go around, so don't be distracted by the rabbits of life. Set your sights on bigger game.

Security and opportunity are total strangers. If an undertaking doesn't include faith, it isn't worthy of being called God's direction. Direction and faith go hand in hand. Those who don't take chances don't make advances. Never waste time planning, analyzing, and risking on small ideas. It's smarter to spend more time on decisions that are irreversible and to spend less time on those that are reversible.

A famous old saying goes like this: "Even a turtle doesn't get ahead unless he sticks his neck out." Dream big because you serve a big God.

Faith Has Feet and Hands

Let's be people who put our faith into action. One individual with faith and action constitutes a majority. Don't wait for your ship to come in; swim to it! Thomas Edison is quoted as saying it best: "Opportunity is missed by most people because it is dressed in overalls and looks like work." True faith has hands and feet; it takes action. It isn't enough to *know* that you know. It's more important to *show* that you know.

Rising above mediocrity never just happens; it's always a result of faith combined with works. Want to be unhappy? Do nothing.

It's 1943 and World War II is raging.

There is a young boy standing at a Jackson, Mississippi, street corner selling newspapers day and night, along with war stamps to support the war effort. He's not afraid of hard work. Born in the charity hospital, he has grown up in the poorest part of town. Both boys who lived across the street from him have already been in and out of jail.

He has no brothers, no sisters, no aunts, no uncles, and his father passed away several years earlier. Since the age of ten, he has been the sole provider for his illiterate mom and himself.

There's a contest across the country to see who can sell the most war stamps. This boy, the most unlikely of success stories, has, over several years, sold twelve million dollars' worth of war stamps! The second place finisher sold four million dollars.

As a result, he wins a trip to meet the president of the United States. With a borrowed suit two sizes too big, he heads off to Washington, DC, for the trip of a lifetime.

Later this young man graduates from Hinds Junior College in Jackson and then serves his country in the Army Reserve. He marries a pretty brunette from Indiana and graduates from Indiana University School of Business.

He goes on to have a successful business career while still being a loving husband, excellent father, and an incredible example. A real success in my eyes. He was the best man at my wedding. The story I'm telling is about my dad, Chester Mason.

I've never met a man who lived more in line with the idea of *Never Give Up* than this man. He had every reason and excuse to quit. But he wouldn't. Not only did this outlook affect his life but it is also impacting generations.

Faith without works is like gold within the earth. It is of no value until it is mined. A person who has faith but no actions is like a bird that has wings but no feet. The Bible says, "Faith by itself, if it does not have works, is dead" (James 2:17 NKJV).

Biblical principles multiplied by nothing equal nothing.

The word *work* appears 564 times in the Bible. It isn't an obscure biblical concept. When faith and works operate together, the result is a masterpiece. We should choose to keep our faith working all the time. George Bernard Shaw said, "When I was young, I observed that nine out of every ten things I did were failures. So I did ten times more work." The faith to move mountains always carries a pick.

When the founder of Holiday Inn, Kemmons Wilson, was asked how he became successful, he replied, "I really don't know why I'm here. I never got a degree, and I've only worked half days my entire life. I guess my advice is to do the same, work half days every day. And it doesn't matter which half. The first twelve hours or the second twelve hours."

Tap into the power that is produced when faith is mixed with action, and then watch what God does in your life.

PART 2

Looking
Outward

Find Yourself
by Giving Yourself
to Others

Some time ago when I answered the phone, the voice on the other end said, "Bang! You're dead!" I paused. I didn't know what to think! Then I heard the familiar voice of James Campbell, a client of mine, saying, "John, just calling to remind you that we need to die to ourselves every day." Wow, what a wake-up call to start the day!

Selfishness always ends in self-destruction. John Ruskin is quoted as saying, "When a man is wrapped up in himself, he makes a pretty small package." There is always room at the top for anyone who is willing to say, "I'll serve," and means it.

Several years ago I was listening to Zig Ziglar. In his presentation he said, "You'll always have everything in life that you want if you'll help enough other people get what they want." When I heard that statement, something went off inside of me. I made a conscious decision to incorporate that concept into my life every day. It has made a tremendous difference.

I am very mindful of this every time I have the privilege of speaking before any audience. I have a ritual that I follow every time I speak. I take time to pray and consider my position as the speaker. I say this: "Lord, I am the lowest person in the room. I am here to serve these people. Help me help them. Please speak through me; use me to help them."

Serving others isn't always the most natural thing to do. We're all conditioned to think of ourselves first. That is why 97 percent of all people will write their own names when offered a new pen to try. Despite our tendency toward self-promotion, it is always true that more is accomplished when nobody cares who gets the credit.

True leadership always begins with servanthood. Be willing to serve without trying to reap the benefits. Before looking for a way to get, look for a way to give.

No one is truly a success in life until he or she has learned how to serve. The old saying is true: "The way to the throne room is through the servants' quarters." One of the most powerful decisions you can make in your life is to do something for someone who does not have the power or resources to return the favor. Our Lord says, "He who is greatest among you shall be your servant" (Matt. 23:11 NKJV). And again He declares: "Whosoever will be great among you, let him be your minister; and whosoever will be chief among you, let him be your servant" (Matt. 20:26–27 KJV).

Being a servant won't make you famous—just rich. When you give of yourself to help others, you cannot help but be abundantly rewarded. The rewards and blessings of service always extend far beyond the scope of this life's rewards. That's true wealth!

It's Better to Be Alone
Than in the Wrong Company

Misery wants your company, but you don't have to give in to it. In Proverbs we read, "A mirror reflects a man's face, but what he is really like is shown by the kind of friends he chooses" (27:19 TLB). Proverbs also tells us, "He who walks with wise men will be wise, but the companion of fools will be destroyed" (13:20 NKJV). We become like those with whom we associate.

A number of years ago I found myself at a stagnation point in my life. I was unproductive and unable to see God's direction clearly. One day I noticed that almost all of my friends were in the same situation. When we got together, our problems were all we talked about. As I prayed about this matter, God showed me that I needed "foundational-level" people in my life. Such people bring out the best in us and influence us to become better. They cause us to have greater faith and confidence and to see things from God's perspective. After being with them, our spirits and our sights are raised.

We need to be careful of the kind of insulation we use in our lives. We need to insulate ourselves from negative people and ideas, but we should never insulate ourselves from godly counsel and wisdom. Your best friends are those who bring out the best in you.

I've found that it is better to be alone than in the wrong company. A single conversation with the right person can be more valuable than years of study. Stay far away from negative-thinking "experts." Remember: in the eyes of average people, average is always considered outstanding. Look carefully at the closest associations in your life; they indicate the direction you're heading.

The Lord showed me that I needed to change my closest associations and meet with some other people on a regular basis. These were men and women of great faith, people who made me a better person when I was around them. They were the ones who saw the gifts in me and could correct me in a constructive, loving way. My choice to change my closest associations was a turning point in my life. My life changed. That day I decided to associate with the right people.

When you surround yourself with the right kind of people, you enter into the God-ordained power of agreement:

> Two can accomplish more than twice as much as one, for the results can be much better. If one falls, the other pulls him up; but if a man falls when he is alone, he's in trouble. And one standing alone can be attacked and defeated, but two can stand back-to-back and conquer; three is even better, for a triple-braided cord is not easily broken. (Eccles. 4:9–10, 12 TLB)

Why Fit In
When You Were Born
to Stand Out?

One of the greatest compliments anyone can give you is to say, "You're different." Christians live in this world, but we are aliens. We're destined for another place; this earth is not our final destination. We should talk differently, act differently, and perform differently. We should stand out, not blend in.

"You are a chosen generation, a royal priesthood, a holy nation, His own special people, that you may proclaim the praises of Him who called you out of darkness into His marvelous light" (1 Pet. 2:9 NKJV). "Don't copy the behavior and customs of this world, but be a new and different person with a fresh newness in all you do and think. Then you will learn from your *own* experience how his ways will really satisfy you" (Rom. 12:2 TLB, italics mine).

There should be something different about you. If you do not stand out in a group, if there is not something unique or different in your life, you should reevaluate yourself. Take a close look at your thoughts, conversations, and actions.

One way to stand head and shoulders above the crowd is to choose to do regular, ordinary things in an extraordinary and supernatural way—with great enthusiasm. God does some of His very best work through people right when the circumstances appear to be stacked against them. In fact, God sided with the underdog—the minority—in every battle described in the Bible.

Majority rule isn't always right. It is usually those without dreams or visions of their own who want to take a vote on everything. People in groups tend to agree on courses of action that they as individuals know aren't right.

Many times the majority is a group of highly motivated snails. If a thousand people say something foolish, it is still foolish. Truth is never dependent upon consensus of opinion.

Don't be persuaded or dissuaded by group opinion. It doesn't make any difference what anyone else believes; *you* must believe.

Be a pioneer! Don't be afraid to get hit with a few arrows! Be who you are, and do what *you* know you should do. As Dr. Seuss asked, "Why fit in when you were born to stand out?"

Never take direction for your personal life from a crowd. Never choose to quit just because somebody disagrees with you. In fact, the two worst things you can say to yourself when you get an idea are: "That's never been tried before, so I can't do it" and "That's been tried before, so I can't do it either!" Someone else's failure in a particular area does not guarantee *your* failure.

Go Through What You've Been Going Through

Stop constantly talking about the situation you're going through. Decide to get through it! Do not accept your present, temporary situation as your permanent condition. Make up your mind to get on with your life and fulfill your divine purpose despite your current circumstances.

Some people stay in the same hopeless place their whole lives, never making a firm decision to seek God and His power in order to get through the circumstances they face. Just because long-suffering is a fruit of the Spirit doesn't mean we are required to stay in a miserable situation one second longer than is absolutely necessary.

God wants each of us to come all the way through whatever situations we face. We are not to be moved by what we see, but by what we do not see. This is what the apostle Paul meant when he wrote that we live by faith, not by sight (2 Cor. 5:7). Today is the day to begin to walk by faith—right out of your present circumstances.

If you've been saying, "I'm going through this situation" for years, you need to change your story. Begin to declare, "I've had enough! Now is the time I'm going to get through this mess!"

Nothing is as it appears. I've learned this to be true about nearly everything.

A woman was flying from Melbourne to Brisbane. Unexpectedly, the plane was diverted to Sydney. The flight attendant explained that there would be a delay, and if the passengers wanted to get off the aircraft, the plane would reboard in fifty minutes. Everybody got off the plane except one lady who was blind. A man had noticed her as he walked by and could tell the lady was blind because her Seeing Eye dog lay quietly underneath the seats in front of her throughout the entire flight. He could also tell she had flown this very flight before because the pilot approached her and, calling her by name, said, "Kathy, we are in Sydney for almost an hour. Would you like to get off and stretch your legs?"

The blind lady replied, "No thanks, but maybe Max would like to stretch his legs."

All the people in the gate area came to a complete standstill when they looked up and saw the pilot walk off the plane with a Seeing Eye dog! The pilot was even wearing sunglasses. People scattered. They not only tried to change planes; they were trying to change airlines!

Things aren't always as they appear. That's why most people stay stuck right where they are and don't break through. Get out of your rut. "Normal is getting dressed in clothes that you buy for work and driving through traffic in a car that you are still paying for—in order to get to the job you need to pay for the clothes and the car, and the house you leave vacant all day so you can afford to live in it" (Ellen Goodman).

The Bible contains many promises that can deliver you today. If you will believe and appropriate these promises, you will see your circumstances line up with the Word and will of God—eventually, if not immediately.

The devil tells us that we will never be victorious, that we will never get through what we are going through. But the Bible tells us:

> No temptation has overtaken you except what is common to mankind. And God is faithful; he will not let you be tempted beyond what you can bear. But when you are tempted, he will also provide a way out so that you can stand up under it. (1 Cor. 10:13)

You should take hold of this verse and use it as scriptural ground to stand on. God is faithful. He will provide a way out for you. You can take your stand of faith and boldly proclaim, "I'm going to get through what I've been going through!" Natural circumstances may still remain unchanged, but between God's efforts and yours, you can know that you are going through that situation.

Here's how we position ourselves to break through: "Do not be conformed to this world, but be transformed by the renewing of your mind, that you may *prove* what is that good and acceptable and perfect will of God" (Rom. 12:2 NKJV, italics mine).

Be transformed by renewing your mind with the Word of God. Then you will know what is the good and perfect will of the Lord, and you will be able to get through—once and for all—what you've been going through for so long.

Say No to Many Good Ideas

One of the devil's tricks is getting us to say yes to too many good things. We end up being spread so thin that we are mediocre in everything and excellent in nothing. The old saying is very true, "There is one guaranteed formula for failure, and that is to try to please everyone."

There comes a time in every one of our lives when we must learn to say no to many good ideas. In fact, the more we grow, the more opportunities we will have to say no to. One key to successful results in life is becoming focused. Nothing brings focus like the word *no*! Perhaps no other key to growth and success is as overlooked as this one. The temptation is always to do a little bit of everything.

The word *no* has power. *No* is an anointed word that can break the yoke of overcommitment and weakness. *No* can be used to turn a situation from bad to good, from wrong to right. Saying no can free you from burdens you don't really need to carry right now. *No* can also allow you to devote the correct amount of attention and effort to God's priorities in your life.

Something that's *good* and something that's *right* aren't always the same thing. The challenge is to discern the difference. It may be good to be a missionary in Iraq, but it may not be right for you. Our responsibility as Christians is always to do the right thing. That must come first. With excellence, we should do the things we're called to do—the things that are right—before we consider anything else.

When you read the title of this nugget, past experiences and present situations probably came to mind. You probably recalled many situations in which "no" or "not right now" would have been the right answer. Don't put yourself through that kind of stress in the future. Learn the power of no.

Say no to these things:

- laziness
- gossip
- blaming others
- worry
- alibis
- wasting time
- complaining
- tardiness
- dishonesty
- criticism
- procrastination

- indecision
- talking more than listening
- complacency
- moodiness
- frowns
- giving up too soon
- anything contrary to the Word of God

Yes and *no* are the two most important words you will ever say. These two words determine your destiny. How and when you say them will affect your entire future.

Remember, saying no to a good idea doesn't mean saying never. "No" may mean "not right now." Saying no to lesser things means saying yes to priorities in your life.

There Are No Shortcuts to Anyplace Worth Going

Do you know that the best shortcut you can ever take is to do what God says in His timing? Shortcuts outside the will of God invite compromise and create strife and confusion.

This old saying is absolutely true: "If you keep your attention on learning the tricks of the trade, you will never learn the trade." Watch out for fads—even spiritual ones—because the letters in *fad* stand for "for a day." There is always free food on a fishhook. We need to understand that we're long-distance runners, not sprinters. As marathoners, we don't need to look for shortcuts that open the door to compromise.

There is a story about a beautiful bird that was known for its great singing. It would sit at the top of a tree and make lovely melodies. One day, a man walking through the woods passed by the tree and heard the beautiful bird. The bird noticed the man and that he was holding a box.

"What do you have in the box?" the bird asked the man.

The man replied that he had large, juicy earthworms in the box. "I will sell you a worm for one of your beautiful feathers," he offered.

The bird pulled out a feather and exchanged it for a worm. He reflected to himself, "Why should I work hard to get worms when it is so easy to get them this way?"

The bird and the man repeated this process over the course of many days, and soon the bird no longer had any beautiful feathers to pay for worms. Furthermore, he could no longer fly, nor was he pretty. He didn't feel like singing beautiful songs, and he was very unhappy.

Like this foolish bird, we are sometimes tempted to look for shortcuts, ways outside of God's will to get ahead and obtain the results we desire. But as the foolish bird learned, there is a price for taking shortcuts.

Eventually, we will learn that there is no shortcut to success. One of the hidden truths of life is that the path to the prize is always more valuable than the prize itself. Shortcuts rob us of valuable lessons we need to learn along the way. Beverly Sills said, "There are no shortcuts to any place worth going."

When you're presented with a shortcut—a way that is not of God—say no. Be persistent and stick to the path where the Lord has placed you. It's the best way to go.

Change the Way You Look at Things and You Yourself Will Change

You are custom-built for change. Created with a capacity to adjust, move, and be different. Nothing remains as constant as change. Even the most precious of all gems needs to be chiseled and faceted to achieve its best luster. Don't end up like concrete—all mixed together and permanently set.

In 1803, the British created a civil service position that required a man to stand on the cliffs of Dover with a spyglass. His duty was to be a lookout against invasion. He was to ring a bell if he saw Napoleon Bonaparte's armies approaching. This job was appropriate at the time, but it wasn't eliminated until 1945! How many "spyglasses on the cliffs of Dover" are we still holding on to in our lives? We shouldn't let the way we are accustomed to doing things interfere with the opportunities God is providing for us today.

When the Lord directs us to change, perhaps we may continue to reach toward the same goal but in a slightly different way. When we refuse to cooperate with the change God requires of us, we make chains of delay that constrain and restrict us.

An inanimate object like an article of clothing doesn't have the ability to truly change; it grows out of style and becomes unusable. But any one of us is able to change at any point in time, at any age. Changing doesn't always mean doing the opposite. In fact, most of the time it means adding to or slightly adjusting what already exists.

Here are three things we know about the future: First, it isn't going to be like the past. Second, it isn't going to be exactly the way we think it's going to be. Third, the rate of change will take place faster than we anticipate. The Bible indicates that in the end times—in which we are now living, I believe—changes will occur more quickly than ever before in history.

In Isaiah the Lord declares: "Behold, the former things have come to pass, and new things I declare; before they spring forth I tell you of them" (42:9 NKJV). The Bible is a book that tells us how to respond to change ahead of time. You see, I believe we can decide in advance how we will respond to most situations. This is a great way to manage and take advantage of changes.

When I was coaching basketball many years ago, I told my players that they could prepare for many situations ahead of time. We used to practice as many gamelike situations as we could so we would already know how to respond when we found ourselves in the actual situations. This one idea helped our teams to be very successful.

One of the main reasons the Bible was written was to prepare us ahead of time, to teach us how to respond in advance to many of the situations we would encounter in life.

Choose to flow with God's plan. Be sensitive to the new things He is doing. Stay flexible to the Holy Spirit, and know that our God directs, adjusts, moves, and corrects us. He is always working to bring us into perfection.

Sometimes the Smallest Step in the Right Direction Is the Biggest Step of Your Life

Every successful person I know is excellent at doing the small things well. When Jesus told the parable of the talents, He referred to a servant who had multiplied his master's money. The master responded to the servant, "Well done, good and faithful servant; you have been faithful over a few things, I will make you ruler over many things. Enter into the joy of your lord" (Matt. 25:23 NKJV). On another occasion, God asks the prophet, "For who has despised the day of small things?" (Zech. 4:10 NKJV). There is power in taking small steps.

Small adds up and goes on to something better. Not unlike the man who said, "If I had a dollar for every girl that found me unattractive, they would eventually find me attractive." Don't be afraid to take small steps. The

Bible promises us that if we are faithful in small matters, one day we will be rulers over many larger things. Many times the impossible is simply the unacted upon small opportunity. Courage grows with each small step you take. Multiplication happens with small steps.

A bunny rabbit was shopping at the supermarket, and a sales assistant said to him, "If you can tell me what 19,866 times 10,543 is, we'll give you free carrots for life."

Immediately, the bunny responded, "209,447,238."

The sales assistant was astonished and asked, "How on earth did you do that?"

The bunny replied, "If there's one thing rabbits are good at, it's multiplying."

Many people aren't moving with God today simply because they were not willing to take the small steps He placed before them. You should leap at the opportunity—no matter how small—to move in the direction the Lord calls you. If you're called to be a youth pastor and are merely sitting at home waiting for an invitation from a large church, it will never come. You need to find the first young person you can, put your arm around him or her, and begin to minister.

I remember a time in my life when I was frozen with fear over what God had called me to do. It seemed so huge a task that I was unable to bring myself to face it. A friend came to me and spoke two words that broke that paralysis in my life. He said, "Do something!" and walked out of my house. That day I "did something." My first small step started momentum in my life, and I began to run toward the vision God had for me. Those two words were a turning point in my life.

If you're at a point of paralysis in your life because of what God wants you to do, my words for you today are "Do something!" Don't worry about the goal; just take the steps that take you past the starting point. Soon you'll get to a point of no return. As you climb higher, you'll be able to see much farther.

As you begin, don't be afraid. Eric Hoffer said, "Fear of becoming a has-been keeps some people from becoming anything." Every great idea is impossible from where you are starting today. But little steps add up, and they add up rapidly. Most people don't succeed because they are too afraid to even try. They don't begin due to the fear of failure.

We should all learn to grow wherever we're planted. Everything big starts with something little. That small action puts you closer to your goal than you were yesterday.

Many times the final goal seems so unreachable that we don't even make an effort. But once you've made your decision and boldly taken a step forward, you're more than halfway there. God will begin with you today—no matter what your circumstances.

Forgive Your Enemies— Nothing Will Annoy Them More

When faced with the need to forgive and forget, never make the excuse, "But no one knows what that person did to me!" That may be true, but do you know what unforgiveness will do to you?

Unforgiveness leads to bitterness, which is a deadly misuse of energy. Pondering a negative situation and plotting how to get even diverts a considerable amount of brain power away from productive thinking. If we keep burning bridges, we'll become isolated and alone, and we'll deal with strangers and enemies the rest of our lives. Let's build bridges, not burn them. What really matters is what happens *in* us, not *to* us. Forgiveness is essential for healthy human relationships. We can't give a hug with our arms folded.

Our forgiveness of others assures us of God's forgiveness of us. Jesus said, "If you forgive other people when they sin against you, your heavenly Father will also forgive you. But if you do not forgive others their sins, your Father will not forgive your sins" (Matt. 6:14–15). The weight of unforgiveness substantially drags us down. It's a tremendous load to carry in the race we're called to run.

Working with churches and businesses throughout America, I have found unforgiveness in every stagnating situation. And conversely, I have found that churches that are growing and prospering talk about future progress, not past problems.

Vengeance is a poor traveling companion. Every Christian is called to a life of reconciliation (2 Cor. 5:18). Trying to get even wastes time and results in unhappiness. God sometimes removes a person from your life; forgive them, but don't run after them.

Never underestimate the power of forgiveness to free you to fulfill your calling. Forgiveness is the one power you have over a person who slanders or criticizes you. The farther you walk in forgiveness, the greater the distance you put between yourself and the negative situation. Life becomes easier when you let go of the forgiveness you never got.

A minister parked his car in a no-parking zone in a large city because he was short on time and couldn't find a space with a meter. So he put a note under the windshield wiper that read, "I have circled the block ten times. If I don't park here, I'll miss my appointment. FORGIVE US OUR TRESPASSES." When he returned, he found a citation from a police officer along with this note: "I've circled this block for ten years. If I don't give you a ticket, I'll lose my job. LEAD US NOT INTO TEMPTATION."

A chip on the shoulder weighs a ton. Instead, travel light. Forgive. It gives you a spring in your walk and a second wind in the race of life.

Sticks and Stones Are Thrown Only at Fruit-Bearing Trees

Nobody can ever make you feel average without your permission. Ingratitude and criticism are going to come as part of the price you'll pay for leaping past mediocrity. So stop letting people who know so little occupy so much of your mind and emotions.

Most of the time, critical people are either jealous or uninformed and say things that have no impact whatsoever upon truth. A famous saying describes this situation perfectly: "It is useless for the sheep to pass resolutions in favor of vegetarianism while the wolf remains of a different opinion."

Be careful what you say about someone else; you never know who you may be talking to. An elderly woman walked into the local country church. The friendly usher greeted her at the door and helped her up the flight of steps. "Where would you like to sit?" he asked politely.

"The front row, please," she answered.

"You really don't want to do that," the usher said. "The pastor is really boring."

"Do you happen to know who I am?" the woman inquired.

"No," he said.

"I'm the pastor's mother," she replied indignantly.

"Do you know who I am?" he asked.

"No," she said.

"Good," he answered.

The Bible offers this great promise concerning criticism: the truth always outlives a lie. This fact is backed by Proverbs. "The truthful lip shall be established forever, but a lying tongue is but for a moment" (12:19 NKJV). We may boldly say, "The Lord is my helper, and I will not fear what man shall do unto me" (Heb. 13:6 KJV)!

After healing the ten lepers, even Jesus Himself was thanked by only one of them, and He was perfect! Don't be surprised by ingratitude.

If you move with God, you will be criticized. The only way to avoid criticism is to do nothing and be nothing. Everyone who gets things done inevitably stirs up criticism. Be bold; get criticized.

Don't respond to criticism; respond to God. Often criticism presents the best platform from which to proclaim the truth.

Never judge people by what their enemies say about them. Kenneth Tynan provides the best description of a critic I've ever heard: "A critic is a man who knows the way but can't drive the car."

If what you say and do is of God, it doesn't make any difference if every other person on the face of the earth criticizes you. Likewise, if what you are doing is not of God, nothing other people say will make it right. Don't let compliments go to your head or criticism to your heart. When you're not attached to praise and criticism, a nearly untouchable freedom comes to your life.

Pay no attention to negative criticism. Instead, "Trust in the Lord, and do good" (Ps. 37:3 NKJV), knowing that in the end what you do in the Lord will be rewarded. Never surrender your dream to noisy negatives.

The Struggle Today Builds Strength for Tomorrow

Every obstacle introduces a person to himself or herself. You find out who you really are and what you genuinely believe in the face of an obstacle. You will find out if what you want is really worth fighting for.

No obstacle leaves you the way it finds you; it changes you for better or worse. It's the way you look at it that makes all the difference. Let each new obstacle take you to the next level in God. Your problem is your promotion.

An excellent example of this in the Bible is the giant obstacle Goliath. He brazenly confronted and intimidated the armies of Israel, including the brothers of a young shepherd named David. We know from history that David's brothers chose not to do anything about the obstacle before them, but David did. Why? The brothers looked at the obstacle and figured it was too big to hit, but David looked at the obstacle and figured it was too big to miss.

Obstacles subdue mediocre people, but great leaders rise above them. You and I need to be like the great man who, when asked what helped him overcome the obstacles of life, responded, "The other obstacles." We should be like a kite that rises *against* the wind.

Many people think most of their obstacles are money related, but the correct perspective is to know that a problem that can be solved with a checkbook is not really an obstacle; it's an expense.

Someone said that obstacles are what we see when we take our eyes off the goal. Keep your eyes on the goal, and remember that you are not alone in your struggle, for "we know that in all things God works for the good of those who love him, who have been called according to his purpose" (Rom. 8:28).

Every obstacle has a limited life span. We worried about things last year that we can't even remember today. Don't believe the devil when he tells you that things will not change, that they will not pass. Every problem has a soft spot.

In times of adversity, you don't have an obstacle; you have a choice. In the midst of unbelievable circumstances, believe. Obstacles don't block the path; they *are* the path. Embrace them, and let them take you higher.

It Takes Little to Follow the Crowd— It Takes Everything to Stand Alone

One day a hunter came across a bear in the woods. The bear said to the hunter, "I want a full stomach."

The hunter responded, "I want a fur coat."

"Let's compromise," suggested the bear, and then he ate the man. As a result, they both got what they wanted. The bear went away with a full stomach, and the man went away wrapped in fur.

That hunter learned the lesson of the wrong kind of compromise. When deciding the lesser of two evils, choose neither. In other words, if in doubt, don't.

When people allow compromise in one area, it always spills over and affects other areas. It opens the door for lies, deceit, and error to creep in and take over. I know people who have turned from the Lord altogether. Their troubles started with compromises. They began to give in to little things, which soon became bigger things. It wasn't long before compromise began to infiltrate their personal lives. Eventually, it overtook and overwhelmed them.

In Proverbs 4 the writer warns us: "Ponder the path of your feet, and let all your ways be established. Do not turn to the right or the left; remove your foot from evil" (vv. 26–27 NKJV). "If you limit your choices to what only seems possible and reasonable, you disconnect yourself from what you truly want, and all that's left is compromise" (Robert Fritz).

In Deuteronomy 30:19 the Lord said to His people, "This day I call the heavens and the earth as witnesses against you that I have set before you life and death, blessings and curses. Now choose life, so that you and your children may live." You and I have a choice. Every day we must choose between life and death. We should never settle for anything; we should always seek the best. It is rarely the strong man who urges compromise. A compromise on what you know is right is more expensive than either of the alternatives.

Don't allow compromise to creep in and destroy. You can't say, "Well, I'll compromise in this one area, and everything else will be okay." Once it has a foothold, compromise grows and spreads. What you compromise, you lose.

God's plan for each of us is for excellence, not mediocrity. If anything is worth doing, it is worth doing well. If you can't do it with excellence, don't bother. Someone asked, "If you don't have time to do it right, when will you have time to do it over?"

Be a person of integrity. Guard your reputation and the reputation of Jesus Christ and His church. If the only way others can tell that you're a Christian is from the fish symbol on your business card, do us all a favor and leave it off. Take a stand today against compromise.

Rise by Lifting Others

I believe every person, no matter how shy, has the potential to lead and influence others. You may never be the president of this organization or that company, but you have influence. Sociologists tell us that even the most introverted person will have contact with more than ten thousand people in their lifetime. Each of these contacts offers a level of influence. In other words, every one of us, even the shy ones, are influencing others every day.

There are ways to lead and influence well. Here are twenty-five of them:

1. Influential leaders launch forth before success is certain.
2. Influential leaders are always full of praise.
3. Influential leaders are people of honesty and integrity.
4. Influential leaders are genuinely interested in others.

5. Influential leaders learn to say "thank you" and "please" on the way to the top.
6. Influential leaders are always growing.
7. Influential leaders are possessed with dreams.
8. Influential leaders are good communicators.
9. Influential leaders are specific about what is expected.
10. Influential leaders hold others accountable.
11. Influential leaders are positive and confident.
12. Influential leaders value results over talk.
13. Influential leaders are unafraid of confrontation.
14. Influential leaders talk about their own mistakes before they talk about someone else's.
15. Influential leaders ask great questions.
16. Influential leaders are quick to praise and encourage the smallest amount of improvement.
17. Influential leaders have good reputations.
18. Influential leaders make others better.
19. Influential leaders make quality decisions.
20. Influential leaders look for and praise someone doing something right.
21. Influential leaders respond to their own failures before others have to reveal them.
22. Influential leaders take others up with them.
23. Influential leaders never allow gossiping from themselves or others.
24. Influential leaders do what is right rather than what is popular.
25. Influential leaders are servants.

Some People Can Live an Entire Month from a Pat on the Back or an Encouraging Word

A famous old poem goes like this:

> When days are hot and flies are thick, use horse
>   sense—cooperate.
> This is a truth all horses know; they learned it
>   many centuries ago.
> One tail on duty at the rear can reach that fly be-
>   hind the ear.
> But two tails, when arranged with proper craft,
>   can do the job both fore and aft.

We should look for opportunities to help each other.

Somebody saw something in you and reached out to help you. That act of kindness determined where you are today. The person may have been your pastor, a parent, a friend, a teacher, a coach, a neighbor, or just someone who gave you extra money, prayers, good advice, or the right equipment and supplies. That individual had the foresight and the resources to invest in you and to take a risk on your future.

William Danforth said, "Our most valuable possessions are those which can be shared without lessening; those which when shared multiply. Our least valuable possessions are those which when divided are diminished."

A verse in Proverbs is one of my favorites. It says, "Do not withhold good from those to whom it is due, when it is in the power of your hand to do so" (3:27 NKJV). You have something in your possession that can bless someone. Maybe it's a timely word, a much-needed piece of advice, a monetary gift to meet a need, or a simple thank-you for a job well done.

I have a challenge for you. Take a few minutes this week and send a note to people who have significantly affected your life. Also, take a few minutes to help someone else get ahead. You will find this to be one of the most satisfying experiences you've had in a long time.

Choosing God's will in our own lives makes those around us better. Invest in somebody today. Believe in that person. Offer support and encouragement. Help that person rise to another level.

Dr. Howard Kelly was a distinguished physician who, in 1895, founded the Johns Hopkins Division of Gynecologic Oncology at Johns Hopkins University. According to the biography *Dr. Kelly of Hopkins: Surgeon, Scientist,*

Christian (Johns Hopkins Press, 1959) by Audrey Davis, on a walking trip up through northern Pennsylvania one spring, Dr. Howard Kelly stopped by a small farmhouse for a drink of cool spring water. A little girl answered his knock and, instead of water, brought him a glass of fresh milk. After a short, friendly visit, he went on his way. Some years later, that same little girl came to him for an operation. Just before she left for home, her bill was brought into the room, and across its face was written in a bold hand, "Paid in full with one glass of milk." There's a saying that goes something like this: "Bread cast on the waters comes back to you. The good deed you do today may benefit you or someone you love at the least expected time. If you never see the deed again at least you will have made the world a better place." And, after all, isn't that what life is all about?

The incredible blessing of helping others comes back to us too. By helping others up you can't help but rise higher yourself. "Whatsoever good thing any man doeth, the same shall he receive of the Lord" (Eph. 6:8 KJV). What you make happen for others, God will make happen for you!

Try it; you'll like it! You'll also benefit from it! And that good thing you've given to others might just come flying back to you too.

Don't Change So People Will Like You— Be Yourself So the Right People Will Love You

In this day of peer pressure, trends, and fads, we need to realize that every person has been custom-made by God the Creator. Each of us has a distinctive purpose. That purpose is to be ourselves. You will never be more in the center of God's will than when you are being exactly the person He created you to be. Yes, *with* all your imperfections and shortcomings but also *with* all the talents and gifts He's given you.

You and I can always find someone richer than we are, poorer than we are, or more or less able than we are. But how other people are, what they have, and what happens in their lives has no effect upon our call. In Galatians we are admonished, "Let everyone be sure that he is doing his very best, for then he will have the personal satisfaction of work well done and won't need to compare himself with someone else" (6:4 TLB).

Our standard is God's unique plan and design for our lives. How the Lord chooses to deal with others has nothing to do with His call for each of us individually. Average people compare themselves with others, but we should always compare ourselves with what God has called us to be and what His Word says.

God made you a certain way. You are unique. You are one of a kind. To copy others is to cheat yourself out of the fullness of what God has called you to be and to do.

Because I do a lot of work with churches and businesses, I come into contact with many different types of people. One time I was talking on the phone with a pastor who I had never met and who did not know me personally. We agreed that I would visit his church as a consultant. As we were closing our conversation and setting a time to meet at the local airport, he asked me, "How will I know you when you get off the plane?"

"Oh, don't worry, Pastor, I'll know you," I responded jokingly. "All you pastors look alike."

Well, wouldn't you know it, he *did not* look like your typical pastor—he had long blond hair, wore jeans, and had a nearly white beard. It took me a while to find him. I'm pretty sure I walked right by him a couple of times before he called my name and introduced himself.

The point of this humorous story is that *you* must be the person God has made *you* to be, not the person others expect or want you to be. Your life was never designed to be a copy. God's plan is unique to you and you alone.

An elderly Chinese woman had two large pots; each hung on the ends of a pole that she carried across her neck. One of the pots had a crack in it while the other pot was perfect and always delivered a full portion of water. At the end of the long walk from the stream to the house, the cracked pot arrived only half full. For a full two years this went on daily, with the woman bringing home only one and a half pots of water.

Of course, the perfect pot was proud of its accomplishments. But the poor cracked pot was ashamed of its own imperfection and miserable that it could only do half of what it had been made to do. After two years of what it perceived to be bitter failure, it spoke to the woman one day by the stream. "I am ashamed of myself, because this crack in my side causes water to leak out all the way back to your house."

The old woman smiled. "Did you notice that there are flowers on your side of the path but not on the other pot's side? That's because I have always known about your flaw, so I planted flower seeds on your side of the path, and every day while we walk back, you water them. For two years I have been able to pick these beautiful flowers to decorate the table. Without you being just the way you are, there would not be this beauty to grace the house."

Each of us has our own unique flaw. But it's the cracks and flaws we each have that make our lives together so very interesting and rewarding. You've just got to take each person for who they are and look for the good in them.

So, to all my fellow crackpots, be yourself, and remember to smell the flowers on your side of the path!

So choose to accept and become the person God has made you to be. Tap into the originality and creative genius of God in your life. There are "flowers" waiting to be watered by you!

Nugget #36

Ten Truisms That Aren't True

1. "Take care of things, and they will take care of you."
   We should not take care; we should take control. If you don't take control of your own life, somebody else will.

2. "If it's not broke, don't fix it."
   Even when things are working, they still can be improved. The temptation with this statement is the so-called safety of the status quo. Status quo is Latin for "the mess we're in."

3. "The way to guarantee success is to work smarter, not harder."
   This is a losing idea. Good work requires you to work smarter *and* work harder. Hard work without smart work will produce mistakes, dead ends, inefficiency, and low levels of results.

4. "Activity equals accomplishment."

Activity is not accomplishment. Hard work is not results. We should not ask ourselves whether we're busy, but what we're busy about. We serve a God who is interested in results.

5. "Never say never."

It's better to say, "Seldom say never and only when you really mean it."

6. "Talk is cheap."

Talk is very expensive. What people say is ultimately what they get and what they pay for. Your words are valuable, not cheap. Life and death are in the power of the tongue.

Two students from Texas and one from Texas Tech are all on death row awaiting execution by electric chair. The first Texas student is strapped to the chair and is asked, "Do you have anything you want to say before we throw the switch?"

And he says, "Yes sir, I just want to say I'm an innocent man."

The warden chuckles a bit to himself, then nods to the man at the switch. The switch is thrown and . . . absolutely nothing happens. The warden is amazed. "Son, the Lord seems to have given you a second chance. Maybe you really *are* innocent. We're gonna let you go free."

The second Texas student is then strapped to the chair. The warden says, "All right, have you got anything to say?"

The student says, "Yes sir. I admit that I did kill that feller, but it was all in self-defense. I never did it in cold blood."

The warden chuckles and nods to the man at the switch, who throws it, and . . . absolutely nothing happens. "Well, I'll be darned," says the warden. "You must be tellin' the truth too! Let 'em go, boys!" And they unstrap him and set him free.

Finally, they bring the Texas Tech student to the chair and strap him in. The warden says, "Now, do *you* have anything to say?"

And the Tech student says, "Sure! If you switched that red wire with that green wire over there, this thing would work!"

Be sure to taste your words before you spit them out.

7. "Don't waste (kill) time."

Although this truism expresses a good thought, it isn't entirely accurate. When you waste your time, you waste your life.

8. "Practice makes perfect."

No, perfect practice makes perfect. Wrong practice leads to wrong habits. Perfect practice leads to perfected action. Make sure that whatever you do on a regular basis is the best you can do.

9. "What you see is what you get."

We Christians are commanded to be moved not by what we see but by the Word of God. We are to see the unseen in every situation. What is unseen many times is more real than what is seen. "Faith is the substance of things hoped for, the evidence of things not seen" (Heb. 11:1 NKJV).

10. "He is a self-made man."

There is no such thing. A person can succeed only with the help of God and others. Everyone needs someone. Egotistical people never get anywhere because they believe they are already there. The truth is, the higher you go in life, the more dependent you become on other people.

PART 3

Looking Upward

Stop Every Day and Look at the Size of God

Who is God? What is His personality? What are His character traits?

According to the Bible, He is everlasting, just, caring, holy, divine, omniscient, omnipotent, omnipresent, and sovereign. He is light, perfection, abundance, salvation, wisdom, and love. He is our creator, savior, deliverer, redeemer, provider, healer, advocate, and friend. Never forget who lives inside you: "The LORD is the great God, the great King above all gods" (Ps. 95:3).

Even though it is humanly impossible to comprehend the immensity of God, we should still lean on his bigness. Isaiah revealed Him this way:

> Who has measured the waters in the hollow of his hand,
> or with the breadth of his hand marked off the heavens?

Who has held the dust of the earth in a basket, or weighed the mountains on the scales and the hills in a balance? . . . He sits enthroned above the circle of the earth, and its people are like grasshoppers. He stretches out the heavens like a canopy, and spreads them out like a tent to live in. (40:12, 22)

Everything you have ever seen above, around, and below is still not a dot in God's vastness. Yet, despite being this large, He still cares for every one of us. He is the one "who desires all men to be saved and to come to the knowledge of the truth" as 1 Timothy 2:4 (NKJV) states, and 2 Peter 3:9 says that He is "not willing that any should perish but that all should come to repentance" (NKJV). God's desire is to have all people rescued and to know Him so He can abundantly bless them with His goodness.

Psalm 147:4 says that God knows how many stars there are and that He has a name for every one of them! But you are much more important to God than the stars. God cares about every detail of your life, and He sees every tear that is cried. He hears every prayer that is prayed, and He never forgets anyone's name.

Jesus taught that even the tiny little sparrows are watched over. "Are not five sparrows sold for two copper coins? And not one of them is forgotten before God. But the very hairs of your head are all numbered. Do not fear therefore; you are of more value than many sparrows" (Luke 12:6–7 NKJV). Think about it! God knows how many hairs are on everyone's head! (And in my case, it's getting easier and easier for Him to count them every year!) Not even one little bird is forgotten by God!

I often travel by air, and one of the benefits is the glimpse I get of God's perspective. I like looking at my challenges from 37,000 feet above the earth. I can see that no problem is too large for God's intervention and marvel that no person is too small for God's attention. Never let the size of your problem determine your size of God. Don't talk about the size of your mountain; talk to the one who can move it.

God is able. If you don't need miracles, you don't need God. My friend Dave Bordon said it best: "I don't understand the situation, but I understand God." It's just dumb not to believe in God and His bigness. I don't know any other way to say it.

An atheist created a case in court against the upcoming Easter and Passover holy days. He hired an attorney to bring a discrimination case against Christians, Jews, and observances of their holy days. The argument was that it was unfair that atheists had no such recognized days.

The case was brought before a judge. After listening to the passionate presentation by the lawyer, the judge banged his gavel, declaring, "Case dismissed!"

The lawyer immediately stood and objected to the ruling, saying, "Your Honor, how can you possibly dismiss this case? The Christians have Christmas, Easter, and others. The Jews have Passover, Yom Kippur, and Hanukkah, yet my client and all other atheists have no such holiday."

The judge leaned forward in his chair and said, "But you do. Your client, counsel, is woefully ignorant. The calendar says April 1 is April Fools' Day. Psalm 14:1 states, 'The fool says in his heart, "There is no God."' Thus, it is the opinion of this court that if your client says there is no God, then he is a fool. Therefore, April 1 is his day. Court is adjourned."

Don't be foolish. What a wonderful, big God we serve. Take time every day to realize it. God is bigger than _____. (Fill in the blank for your own life.)

Ideas Go Away, but Direction Stays

How do you know the difference between ideas that come to your mind and direction from God? There is a persistence to direction. The Bible says, "Many are the plans in a person's heart, but it is the LORD's purpose that prevails" (Prov. 19:21). In Psalm 32 the Lord promises, "I will instruct you and teach you in the way you should go; I will guide you with My eye" (v. 8 NKJV).

Direction is the mother of divine discomfort. Divine discomfort is a sense that God wants to direct us, a stirring so that we are never completely satisfied with where we are in God or what we're doing for Him. If you think you've "arrived" with God, beware. There is always room for growth.

Be aware of areas *out* of which God is calling you and *into* which He is calling you. There is a difference between God's will *in* our lives and God's will *for* our lives. God's will for our lives includes those things that He intends for every person—salvation, strength, health, peace, joy, and other good things. But God's will in our lives is unique to each individual. One person may be called to live in one place for life while another is called to move six times within ten years.

Direction is a stream with banks. It keeps us from wandering aimlessly and spilling into areas we don't need to be involved in. When we know what God wants us to do, then we can have total confidence that what we are attempting is right and that God is on our side. Direction is a matter of fact; ideas are a matter of opinion. Direction from God is impossible to follow without His involvement.

We should be known as a people with a mission, not as a people just fishin'. Evangelist R. W. Schambach put it this way: "Be called and sent, not up and went." We are a people with a purpose, not a problem. "God will never leave you empty. He will replace everything you've lost. If He asks you to put something down, it's because He wants you to pick up something better" (Anonymous).

The apostle Paul wrote to the Colossians, "[Give] thanks to the Father who has qualified us to be partakers of the inheritance of the saints in the light. He has delivered us from the power of darkness and conveyed us into the kingdom of the Son of His love" (1:12–13 NKJV).

Never be afraid of the light of God's direction. Maurice Freehill asked, "Who is more foolish, a child afraid of the dark or the man afraid of the light?" Wherever God guides, He provides. And whom God calls, He appoints and anoints to do the work.

Lay hold of those persistent directions in your life, and tap into the power of God's will for you.

Go Away to Get Ahead

Sometimes the most important thing we can do is get away to a peaceful, God-filled spot. Retreat to advance. Every now and then, you need to leave certain feelings and thoughts behind.

There are times when we should not see people; times when we should direct our whole attention toward God. I believe that we should have a place of refuge, a place out of the normal scope of living, a place where we can be alone and focus on the Lord. When we draw away for a time, we can see and hear much more clearly how to go ahead. Jesus did this many times during His earthly life, especially just before and after major decisions. The Bible says, "In quietness and confidence shall be your strength" (Isa. 30:15 NKJV). There's something invigorating and renewing about retreating to a quiet place of rest and peace. Silence is an environment in which great ideas are birthed.

This is one of the most powerful concepts I have incorporated into my life. I've spent many hours writing books in a cabin on a hill overlooking a beautiful lake, miles away from the nearest city; at a Florida resort; in a hotel suite; or late at night all alone at my office.

Where is that spot for you? It may be a particular room in your home, a spot on a nearby lake, or maybe at the back of the sanctuary of your church. It's somewhere you don't normally spend much time. Make a regular appointment with yourself; it will be one of the most important appointments you keep during the course of a week or a month.

Intently associate with your loftiest dreams as often as you can. Find a place where you can do that in privacy and comfort. In Isaiah we read, "But those who wait on the LORD shall renew their strength; they shall mount up with wings like eagles, they shall run and not be weary, they shall walk and not faint" (40:31 NKJV). Learn to wait upon the Lord. See how much further you move forward with God as a result.

Knowing What God Cannot Do Reveals What He Can Do

1. God cannot leave us or forsake us.
2. God cannot go back on His promises.
3. God cannot be the author of confusion.
4. God cannot revoke His gifts.
5. God cannot be mocked. A man will reap what he sows.
6. God cannot prefer one person over another.
7. God cannot recall our sins after we've asked for forgiveness.
8. God cannot be defeated.
9. God cannot alter the past. (Though politicians try!)
10. God cannot be too big for our problems.
11. God cannot be too little for our problems.
12. God cannot break His covenant.

13. God cannot revoke His calling.

14. God cannot be unjust.

15. God cannot change.

16. God cannot be late.

17. God cannot be neutral.

18. God cannot be weak.

19. God cannot lie.

20. God cannot do anything contrary to Scripture.

21. God cannot bless a lie.

22. God cannot love sin.

23. God cannot withhold wisdom from those who ask in faith.

24. God cannot be pleased without faith.

25. God cannot give anything to a double-minded man.

26. God cannot give us peace and happiness apart from Himself.

27. God cannot be forced into an impossible situation.

28. God cannot be our problem.

29. God cannot be overcome by the world.

30. God cannot bless doubt.

31. God cannot ignore the praises of His people.

Just Say Yes

When you say yes to God unconditionally, you have no idea where that yes will take you. I promise you will go beyond your wildest imagination to places and people you never could have encountered otherwise.

Acting on God's will is like riding a bicycle; if you don't keep moving you fall off! "Saying 'yes' to God is not about perfect performance, but about perfect surrender to the Lord day-by-day" (Lysa TerKeurst).

A famous saying holds that people can be divided into three groups: (1) those who make things happen; (2) those who watch things happen; and (3) those who wonder what's happening. Most people miss out on God's best in their lives because they aren't prepared. The Bible advises us to be prepared continually. The apostle Paul exhorts us to "be ready in season and out of season" (2 Tim. 4:2 NKJV). Proverbs 16:9 puts it this way, "The mind of a man plans his way, But the Lord shows him what to do" (NLV).

Now when I am stuck in traffic, miss an elevator, turn back to answer a call, or encounter any of the little things that annoy me, I think, *Maybe this is exactly where God wants me to be at this very moment.*

The next time your morning seems to be going wrong, the children are slow getting dressed, you can't seem to find the car keys, and you hit every traffic light, don't get mad or frustrated; God is at work watching over you.

May God continue to bless you with all those annoying little things—and may you remember and appreciate their possible purpose. Be ready! He wants to direct your path at the right time in the best direction. Sometimes in the most unusual ways. Ours is a God of velocity. Velocity is all about timing and direction. Since these two always go together, it's never wise to act upon only one without the other.

A police officer radioed the police station.

"I have an interesting case here. An elderly lady just shot her husband for stepping on the floor she just mopped."

"Well . . . have you arrested the woman?"

"Not yet. The floor's still wet."

Jumping at the first opportunity seldom leads to a happy landing. In this proverb, Solomon tells us, "Do not go out in a hurry to argue. Or what will you do in the end, when your neighbor puts you to shame?" (Prov. 25:8 NLV). Even the right direction taken at the wrong time is a bad decision.

Once we know God's will and timing, we should instantly obey, taking action without delay. I have found this to be true: the longer we take to act on whatever God wants us to do, the more unclear His directives become. When God is telling us to do something now, delay is sin. We need to make sure we're on God's straight and narrow road, not in a cul-de-sac.

So, say yes to God now. Seek His timing and direction. When you find both and act accordingly, you'll find yourself right where He wants you to be. It's the only place to be.

The Bible Is a Book
of Directions, Not Suggestions

1. To follow the rule of peace (Col. 3:15)
2. To have no fear of what man can do to us (Luke 12:4)
3. To be abounding, steadfast, and immovable (1 Cor. 15:58 NKJV)
4. To be in right relationship with our friends (Matt. 5:23–24)
5. Not to get even (1 Thess. 5:15)
6. To be an example to others (1 Tim. 4:12)
7. To renew our minds (Rom. 12:2)
8. To avoid wrong conversation (1 Tim. 6:20)
9. To separate ourselves from unclean things (2 Cor. 6:17)
10. To be content with what we have (Heb. 13:5)

11. To avoid murmuring and disputing (Phil. 2:14 KJV)
12. To be filled with the Spirit (Eph. 5:18)
13. To honor our parents (Eph. 6:2; Matt. 19:19)
14. Not to be like the world (Rom. 12:2)
15. To avoid greed and envy (Heb. 13:5)
16. To resist the devil (James 4:7)
17. To put on the whole armor of God (Eph. 6:11)
18. To be patient with all people (1 Thess. 5:14)
19. To be people of quality (Heb. 6:12)
20. To teach our children about the Lord (Eph. 6:4)
21. Not to quit (2 Thess. 3:13)
22. To beware of false prophets (Matt. 7:15)
23. Not to quench the Spirit (1 Thess. 5:19)
24. To humble ourselves (James 4:10)
25. To abstain from all lust of the flesh (1 Pet. 2:11)
26. To cast all our cares upon the Lord (1 Pet. 5:7)
27. To come boldly to God (Heb. 4:16)
28. To give thanks in everything (1 Thess. 5:18)
29. To give no place to the devil (Eph. 4:27)
30. Not to grieve the Holy Spirit (Eph. 4:30)
31. To submit ourselves to God (James 4:7)
32. To let men see our good works (Matt. 5:16)
33. To walk in the Spirit (Gal. 5:25)
34. To cast down vain imaginations (2 Cor. 10:5 KJV)
35. To worship decently and in order (1 Cor. 14:40)
36. Not to forsake assembling with others (Heb. 10:25)
37. To look to Jesus (Heb. 12:2)
38. Not to be ashamed of the gospel of Jesus (Rom. 1:16)

39. To be in agreement (Matt. 18:19)

40. Not to cause others to stumble (Rom. 14:13)

41. To bless those who persecute us (Matt. 5:44)

42. To redeem the time (Eph. 5:16 NKJV)

43. To have confidence in God (Heb. 10:35)

44. To do all to God's glory (1 Cor. 10:31)

45. To seek God's kingdom and righteousness (Matt. 6:33)

Perhaps this story from Robert Ketcham's book, *I Shall Not Want*, instructs us best:

> A Sunday School teacher asked her group of children if anyone could quote the entire Twenty-third Psalm. A golden-haired, four-and-a-half-year-old girl was among those who raised their hands.
>
> A bit skeptical, the teacher asked if she could actually quote the entire psalm.
>
> The little girl came to the front of the room, faced the class, made a perky little bow, and said, "The Lord is my shepherd, that's all I want."
>
> She bowed again and went and sat down. That may be the greatest interpretation of the Twenty-third Psalm ever heard.

God's instructions are there for us to help us, guide us, and express His love for us.

To Listen to God's Voice, Turn Down the World's Volume

We need to be sensitive to what lies in the unseen. Not realizing what lay just beneath their feet, many people have walked right over rich pools of oil or veins of gold. Their vision was too limited. They saw only the ground, not the treasure hidden in it.

The only safe way to decide which direction to go is to distinguish between the voices we hear: God's, our own, and the devil's. Learn to differentiate between these three to eliminate foggy areas in life that blind you. This skill is a key to being able to see and think clearly. Like natural fog, spiritual fog is very dangerous to drive through. Stay in the clear by knowing what God's Word says. It perfectly reflects His voice and helps you discern whether words from other sources are true.

Every good opportunity that presents itself isn't necessarily God's will for us. Many times circumstances line up and everything looks good, yet the opportunity doesn't seem right. That is why we hear from God. I've discovered that divine direction is found by listening to God's still, small voice.

We should build on what we hear on the inside, not on what we see on the outside. There's a big difference between having an ability to do something and being called and anointed to do it. You may have seen someone in church who has an ability to sing, but that talent isn't necessarily evidence that the person has been called by God to the life of a singer. A gift is not a calling.

I am not suggesting that God isn't directing us to use our abilities. But ability shouldn't be the only criteria for deciding whether we make a particular choice. Not only does the Lord give us a road map, but He also provides direction signals, information signs, a vehicle, fuel, and divine direction.

We should be more interested in the unseen than in the seen. When I get my focus off of what I see, read, listen to, and watch, I can hear God speaking to my heart so much more clearly. "Listen to God's voice in everything you do and everywhere you go; He's the one who will keep you on track" (Prov. 3:6 MSG).

God whispers in our souls and speaks to our hearts. It's our choice to listen or not.

Look beyond what you see with your natural eyes. Listen with your spiritual ears. Keep your antenna up for God's perfect direction in your life.

A Moment in God's Presence Can Change a Whole Story

Yes, God wants to bless you, but He also wants you to experience His presence. Jesus said, "My peace I give to you" (John 14:27 NKJV). You'll find great peace and rest in the presence of God. Trouble, nervousness, anxiety, unrest—all these flee in the presence of the Lord.

Something wonderful happens every time you experience the presence of God. You receive joy. In Psalm 16:11 David said of the Lord, "You will fill me with joy in your presence, with eternal pleasures at your right hand." We can't help but experience great joy in our lives when we're in the presence of the Lord.

In Psalm 89:15 we read, "Blessed are those who have learned to acclaim you, who walk in the light of your presence, LORD." Wherever God is, there is great illumination. If there is a dark area in your life, an area in which you are having difficulty seeing clearly, invite the presence of the Lord into that area. If you're having problems with your work, invite God to your job. If you're having difficulty at home, invite God into your home. The mere presence of God will bring illumination and cause all darkness to leave. It will shed great light on your path.

You receive God's divine protection. "You shall hide them in the secret place of Your presence from the plots of man; You shall keep them secretly in a pavilion from the strife of tongues" (Ps. 31:20 NKJV). Thank God for His divine protection and shelter in our lives! Everyone needs a hiding place, a place of safety and refuge.

The presence of God provides a shelter to keep us from evil plans and words. When you're troubled by the actions and words of others, invite God's presence into those circumstances. He will be a shelter, a hiding place for you. Even when we don't sense His presence, His loving care is all around us.

Invite God's presence everywhere you are. James 4:8 promises, "Come near to God and he will come near to you." He will encamp around you every minute and be with you in every situation of life. In His presence you will find great joy and light, divine protection, peace, and rest.

You Can Buy an Education but Wisdom Comes from God

Expect wisdom from God. He's very willing to give it to you.

The Bible says, "If any of you lacks wisdom, let him ask of God, who gives to all liberally and without reproach, and it will be given to him" (James 1:5 NKJV).

We have available to us the wisdom of the Creator of the universe. So few drink at the fountain of His wisdom; most just rinse out their mouths. Many try to live without the wisdom of the Bread of Life, but they will die in their efforts.

Wisdom is seeing everything from God's perspective. It is knowing when and how to use the knowledge that comes from the Lord. An old adage says, "He who knows nothing, doubts nothing." I say, he who knows the truth has a solid basis for his belief.

When you've heard God's voice, you've heard His wisdom. Thank God for His mighty wisdom; it forces a passage through the strongest barriers.

The world doesn't spend billions of dollars for wisdom; it spends billions in search of wisdom. You can buy education, but wisdom comes from God. It's readily available to everyone who seeks its divine source.

Here are eleven ways to gain godly wisdom:

1. Know God's Word (Josh. 1:8).
2. Fear God (Ps. 111:10).
3. Hear God (Prov. 2:6).
4. Receive God's correction (Prov. 3:12).
5. Look to God (Prov. 3:13).
6. Choose God's way (Prov. 8:10–11).
7. Be humble before God (Prov. 11:2).
8. Take God's advice (Prov. 13:10).
9. Please God (Eccles. 2:26).
10. Know the Son of God (1 Cor. 1:30).
11. Pray to God (Eph. 1:16–17).

There is always a wise solution to every situation and opportunity you face.

Many years ago in a small Indian village, a farmer had the misfortune of owing a large sum of money to a local moneylender.

The moneylender, who was old and ugly, fancied the farmer's beautiful daughter. So he proposed a bargain. He said he would forgive the farmer's debt if he could marry his daughter.

Both the farmer and his daughter were horrified by the proposal. So the cunning moneylender suggested that they let providence decide the matter. He told them that he would put a black pebble and a white pebble into an empty money bag. Then the girl would have to pick one pebble from the bag.

1. If she picked the black pebble, she would become his wife and her father's debt would be forgiven.
2. If she picked the white pebble, she need not marry him and her father's debt would still be forgiven.
3. But if she refused to pick a pebble, her father would be thrown into jail.

They were standing on a pebble-strewn path in the farmer's field. As they talked, the moneylender bent over to pick up two pebbles. As he picked them up, the sharp-eyed girl noticed that he had picked up two black pebbles and put them into the bag. He then asked the girl to pick a pebble from the bag.

The girl at first thought there were only three possibilities:

1. The girl should refuse to take a pebble.
2. The girl should show that there were two black pebbles in the bag and expose the moneylender as a cheat.
3. The girl should pick a black pebble and sacrifice herself in order to save her father from his debt and imprisonment.

She did the only thing she knew to do. She quietly prayed and asked God for wisdom. At the same time, she determined to take whatever action He directed her to take. Then a wise idea came to her.

The girl put her hand into the money bag and drew out a pebble. Without looking at it, she fumbled and let it fall onto the pebble-strewn path where it immediately became lost among all the other pebbles.

"Oh, how clumsy of me," she said. "But never mind; if you look into the bag for the one that is left, you will be able to tell which pebble I picked."

Since the remaining pebble was black, it must be assumed that she had picked the white one. And since the moneylender dared not admit his dishonesty, the girl changed what seemed like an impossible situation into an extremely advantageous one. Wisdom won.

Whatever you need, God's wisdom is there for you.

Prayer—The World's Greatest Wireless Communication

One of my favorite prayers is only one word: *Help!* "Help, help, help!" I believe God hears so much more than that one word. All our worries, thoughts, hopes, and dreams are wrapped up in that petition. He already knows what's in our hearts before we pray.

The strongest action you can take in any situation is to go to your knees and ask God for help. You stand tallest when you're on your knees. Whatever is worth worrying about is certainly worth praying about. Prayer unlocks God's treasure chest of great ideas.

When you pray, listen and be simultaneously willing to take the action that God directs in answer to your prayer. He will direct your steps. I've discovered that many answers to our prayers are found in the action He leads us to take.

There are many kinds of prayers, but here are five that I find myself praying:

1. Conversation: "Good morning, Father."
2. Praise and thanksgiving: "Thanks, Lord!"
3. Petition: "Father, I need."
4. Intercession: "God, help."
5. Forgiveness: "Father, I confess my sin. I ask for Your forgiveness and request that You cleanse me from all unrighteousness."

In Philippians 4:6–7 the apostle Paul counsels us, "Do not be anxious about anything, but in every situation, by prayer and petition, with thanksgiving, present your requests to God. And the peace of God, which transcends all understanding, will guard your hearts and your minds in Christ Jesus." And in Colossians 4:2 he says, "Devote yourselves to prayer, being watchful and thankful."

Here are twelve benefits of prayer:

1. Prayer brings the right things to pass (Matt. 7:7–11).
2. Prayer sends laborers into the harvest (Matt. 9:38).
3. Prayer defeats the devil (Matt. 17:21).
4. Prayer overcomes the impossible (Matt. 21:22).
5. Prayer guards against temptation (Matt. 26:41).
6. Prayer reveals God's answers (Luke 11:9–10).
7. Prayer saves the unbeliever (Acts 2:21).
8. Prayer brings peace (Phil. 4:5–7).
9. Prayer imparts wisdom (James 1:5).
10. Prayer heals the sick (James 5:13–15).

11. Prayer changes the natural (James 5:17–18).

12. Prayer edifies the believer (Jude v. 20).

Be honest with God. He knows your prayers and thoughts before you say them.

A four-year-old boy was asked to return thanks before Christmas dinner. The family members bowed their heads in expectation. He began his prayer, thanking God for all his friends, naming them one by one.

Then he thanked God for Mommy, Daddy, brother, sister, Grandma, Grandpa, and all his aunts and uncles. Then he began to thank God for the food. He gave thanks for the turkey, the dressing, the fruit salad, the cranberry sauce, the pies, the cakes, even the Cool Whip. Then he paused, and everyone waited—and waited.

After a long silence, the young fellow looked up at his mother and asked, "If I thank God for the broccoli, won't He know that I'm lying?"

"Honest to God" is a good way to live and pray.

If you only pray when you're in trouble—you're in trouble. You will discover that God speaks to those who listen and listens to those who pray. Prayer changes everything.

God Speaks—
Are You Listening?

Hearing something is of little value; we must listen in order to understand. Unfortunately, one of our least developed skills is listening. There are really two different kinds of listening. There is human listening, which is interaction with other people, and there is spiritual listening, which is interaction with God.

It has been said, "Men are born with two ears but only one tongue, which indicates that they were meant to listen twice as much as they talk." In human communication, leaders should always monopolize the listening. What we learn about another person will always result in a greater reward than what we tell him or her about ourselves.

Sam feared that his wife, Judy, wasn't listening as well as she used to, and he thought she might need a hearing aid. Not quite sure how to approach her, he called the family doctor to discuss the problem.

The doctor told him there was a simple, informal test the husband could perform to give the doctor a better idea about her hearing loss.

"Here's what you do," said the doctor. "Stand about forty feet away from her, and in a normal conversational speaking tone, say something and see if she hears you. If not, go to thirty feet, then twenty feet, and so on until you get a response."

That evening, his wife was in the kitchen cooking dinner, and he was in the living room. He said to himself, "I'm about forty feet away. Let's see what happens." Then in a normal tone, he asked, "Honey, what's for dinner?" No response.

So Sam moved closer to the kitchen, about thirty feet from his wife, and repeated, "Judy, what's for dinner?" Still no response. Next, he moved into the dining room where he was about twenty feet from his wife and asked, "Sweetie, what's for dinner?" Again he got no response.

So he walked up to the kitchen door, about ten feet away. "Honey, what's for dinner?" Again there was no response. So he walked right up behind her. "Judy, what's for dinner?"

"For Pete's sake, Sam, for the *fifth* time, *chicken!*"

Sometimes we think others aren't listening when we are the ones who aren't. Listening is our responsibility in our relationships with others and with God.

Regarding spiritual listening, Proverbs 8:34–35 quotes the persona of Wisdom, who says, "Blessed are those who listen to me, watching daily at my doors, waiting at my doorway. For those who find me find life and receive favor from the Lord."

Valuable wisdom and supernatural favor are to be gained by listening.

Look at the results of spiritual hearing *and* listening that we see in Luke 8:15. This passage relates to the parable of the sower: "The seed on good soil stands for those with a noble and good heart, who hear the word, retain it, and by persevering produce a crop." Harvest is associated not only with persevering and good seed in good soil, but also with those people who hear the Word of God and retain it. You can only retain what you learn by listening to what you hear.

Proverbs 15:31 says, "Whoever heeds life-giving correction will be at home among the wise." Listening allows us to maintain a teachable spirit. Listening increases our teachability. Those who give us life-giving rebukes can be great blessings to us.

The Bible teaches that we are to be quick to listen and slow to speak (James 1:19). We must never listen passively, especially to God. If we resist hearing, a hardening can take place in our lives. Callousness can develop. In Luke 16:31 Jesus said of a particular group of people, "If they do not listen to Moses and the Prophets, they will not be convinced even if someone rises from the dead." The more we resist listening to the voice of God, the less fine-tuned our hearing becomes.

We need to learn to listen and observe aggressively. Hearing tells you the music is playing; listening tells you what the song is saying. We must try harder to truly listen, not just hear.

Fine-tune your natural and spiritual ears to listen and learn.

God Is Not Your Problem— He's Your Answer

Some time ago I was eating at a Mexican fast-food restaurant. As I stood in line for service, I noticed in front of me an elderly lady who looked like she might have been homeless. I concluded this because she was carrying a grocery bag filled to the top with what seemed like all of her possessions in the world. When it was her turn to order, she asked for a drink of water and one taco.

I couldn't help but observe her and be moved with compassion for her. Shortly after I began my meal, I walked over to her and asked if I could buy her some more food to eat. She looked at me and angrily said, "Who are you?"

"Just a guy who wants to help," I responded.

She ignored me, so I sat back down in my booth. We both finished our meals and got up to leave at about the same time. As she began to walk out of the restaurant, I followed her because I felt led to give her some money. In the parking lot, I approached her and offered her some cash.

Her only response was, "Stop bothering me!" Then she stormed off.

Immediately, the Lord spoke this to my heart: "That's the way my people respond to me."

God is up in heaven wanting to pour out a blessing, and we respond by saying, "Who are You? What do You want from me?" The Lord, being the gracious God that He is, continues to try to bless us. Yet we react by saying, "Stop bothering me! I'll do this myself." Missing out on the abundant blessings of the Lord, we walk away, just as this lady did.

It isn't the absence of problems that gives us peace; it's God who is with us in the problems. In Romans 8:38–39 the apostle Paul wrote, "For I am convinced that neither death nor life, neither angels nor demons, neither the present nor the future, nor any powers, neither height nor depth, nor anything else in all creation, will be able to separate us from the love of God that is in Christ Jesus our Lord." In verse 31 he declared, "What, then, shall we say in response to these things? If God is for us, who can be against us?" A paraphrase might be, "If God is for us, who cares who is against us?"

Thank God that we can, without hesitation and with full confidence, lean on His eternal faithfulness.

Learn the Alphabet for Success

A Action

B Belief

C Commitment

D Direction

E Enthusiasm

F Faith

G Goals

H Happiness

I Inspiration

J Judgment

K Knowledge

L Love

M Motivation

N Nonconformity

O Obedience

P Persistence

Q Quality

R Righteousness

S Steadfastness

T Thankfulness

U Uniqueness

V Vision

W Wisdom

X (E)xcellence

Y Yieldedness

Z Zeal

Develop a Holy Curiosity That God Is Always Up to Something in Your Life

The measure of a person is not in what they do on Sunday but in who they are Monday through Saturday. God wants you to walk every day in the same closeness, strength, joy, and direction you experience with Him on Sunday. You don't have to leave that atmosphere. God is with you—period. Every day. The devil wants to ambush you by bringing to your mind thoughts of fear, doubt, unbelief, and destruction.

Our inner self is always willing, but our humanity resists. That's what Jesus meant when He said to His disciples, "Watch and pray, lest you enter into temptation. The spirit indeed is willing, but the flesh is weak" (Matt. 26:41 NKJV).

The advantage of walking in the Spirit is that it keeps us on the right path. In Galatians 5:16 the apostle Paul

writes, "So I say, walk by the Spirit, and you will not grat-
ify the desires of the flesh." Let's guard our minds and
hearts. As spiritual creatures, we walk by faith, not by
sight (2 Cor. 5:7). We are commanded to live in the Spirit,
not in selfish human desires.

People whose eyes, ears, and minds are directed
toward the world find it difficult to hear God speaking
to them. The Lord wants to talk to you at work, at lunch,
at play—everywhere you go. Some of my greatest revela-
tions from God have come not in my prayer closet but
in the midst of my everyday life, while doing normal,
everyday things.

I remember vividly a day when God clearly spoke to my
heart. I was doing a very normal, everyday thing—driving
my car on the highway outside of Tulsa, Oklahoma. As I
was minding my own business, I sincerely felt the Lord
speak to my heart. This is what I heard: "John, I want you
to do three things with your life and ministry. First, you will
discern the truth from the lie. Second, you will be a divine
connection for people. And third, you will see the gifts
and talents in others, and what you do will stir them up."

Every single one of these three directives has been
operating in my life ever since. Again, I was just minding
my own business driving down the road. Little did I expect
to have one of the most significant spiritual encounters
of my life. But I was open to whatever God wanted me to
do, wherever he wanted me to go, however he wanted
to show me.

Thank God that our relationship with Him is not a
sometimes affair; it's an all-the-time union! With the
words of the old hymn, I say, "He leadeth me! O blessed
thought!" God is with you!

Nugget #51

God Will Use You
Right Where You Are Today

Y ou don't need to do anything else for God to begin
to use you now. You don't need to read another
book, listen to another teaching, memorize another Scripture, plant another financial gift, or repeat
another creed or confession. You don't even need to attend another church service before God can begin to
make use of you.

God uses willing vessels, not brimming vessels. And
He's never had anyone "qualified" working for Him.
Throughout the Bible, in order to fulfill His plans for the
earth, God used people from all walks of life, with all
their faults and strengths:

1. Abraham, a nomad who became the father of many
nations

2. Jacob, a deceiver who became the father of the twelve tribes of Israel and whose name became Israel

3. Joseph, a prisoner who became prime minister

4. Moses, a stutterer who became a deliverer

5. Aaron, a servant who became God's spokesman

6. Joshua, an assistant who became a conqueror

7. Deborah, a housewife who became a judge

8. Gideon, a common laborer who became a valiant leader of men

9. David, a shepherd boy who became a king

10. Elijah, an ordinary man who became a mighty prophet

11. Hezekiah, an idolatrous father's son who became a king renowned for doing right in the sight of the Lord

12. Nehemiah, a cupbearer who built the wall of Jerusalem

13. Esther, an orphan who became a queen

14. Isaiah, a man of unclean lips who prophesied the birth of God's Messiah

15. Jeremiah, a child who fearlessly spoke the Word of the Lord

16. Shadrach, Meshach, and Abednego, Hebrew exiles who became great leaders of the nation of Babylon

17. Hosea, a marital failure who prophesied to save Israel

18. Matthew, a government employee who became an apostle

19. John the Baptist, a vagabond who became the fore-runner of Jesus

20. Mary, an unknown virgin who gave birth to the Son of God

21. James and John, fishermen who became close disciples of Christ and were known as "sons of thunder"

22. Peter, a businessman who became a great evangelist

23. Nicodemus, a Pharisee who became a defender of the faith

24. Paul, a persecutor who became the greatest missionary in history and the author of two-thirds of the New Testament

All God needs is all of you!

John Mason is a national bestselling author, minister, executive author coach, and noted speaker. He's the founder and president of Insight International and Insight Publishing Group, organizations dedicated to helping people reach their dreams and fulfill their God-given destinies.

He has authored nineteen books, including *An Enemy Called Average*, *You're Born an Original—Don't Die a Copy*, *Let Go of Whatever Makes You Stop*, and *Know Your Limits— Then Ignore Them*. Mason's books have sold nearly two million copies and are translated into thirty-eight languages throughout the world. His books are widely respected as a source of godly wisdom, scriptural motivation, and practical principles. His writings have twice been published in *Reader's Digest* along with numerous other national publications. Six of his books have reached the #1 spot on Amazon bestseller lists. Known for his quick wit, powerful thoughts, and insightful ideas, he is a popular speaker across the United States and around the world.

John and his wife, Linda, have four children: Michelle, Greg, Michael, and David, and three grandchildren: Emma, Olivia, and Beckett. They all reside in Tulsa, Oklahoma.

John welcomes the opportunity to speak at your organization's events, conferences, or services. He also offers individual author coaching and book development services. If you want more information about speaking or are considering writing a book, contact the Insight office for more information.

Insight International Inc. / Insight Publishing Group

www.freshword.com
contact@freshword.com

Find More Wisdom from
John Mason

freshword.com |

You Were Created to Make a Difference

You were created
on purpose, *for* a purpose.

Everyone can be successful in life—no exceptions. John Mason shows you how to believe it and live it with fifty-two nuggets of truth that bust down the barriers of unfulfilled dreams and release you to become all that God created you to be.